Taming a Liger

Taming a Liger

Unexpected Spiritual
Lessons from
NAPOLEON DYNAMITE

Jeff Dunn & Adam Palmer

Th1nk Books
an imprint of NavPress®

TH1NK
P.O. Box 35001
Colorado Springs, Colorado 80935

TH1NK is an imprint of NavPress.
TH1NK and the TH1NK logo are registered trademarks of NavPress. Absence of ® in
connection with marks of NavPress or other parties does not indicate an absence of registration
of those marks.

ISBN 1-57683-910-9

Cover design by Disciple Design
Cover photo by Phillip Parker
Illustrations by Steve Parolini
Creative Team: Nicci Jordan, Darla Hightower, Arvid Wallen, Steve Parolini, Glynese Northam

Dunn, Jeff, 1959-
   Taming a liger : unexpected spiritual lessons from Napoleon Dynamite /
Jeff Dunn and Adam Palmer.
     p. cm.
   Includes bibliographical references and index.
   ISBN 1-57683-910-9 (alk. paper)
   1. Christian teenagers--Religious life. 2. Napoleon Dynamite (Motion
picture) I. Palmer, Adam, 1975- II. Title.
   BV4531.3.D85 2005
   248.8'3--dc22

                        2005011622

3 4 5 6 7 8 9 10 11 / 09 08 07 06 05

FOR A FREE CATALOG OF
NAVPRESS BOOKS & BIBLE STUDIES,
CALL 1-800-366-7788 (USA)
OR 1-800-839-4769 (CANADA)

CONTENTS

INTRODUCTION

INTRODUCING
TAMING A LIGER

If you're a skeptic, like we are, you're probably looking at this book thinking, *You've got to be kidding me. They actually published a book about* Napoleon Dynamite. *It's just a stupid movie. It's not about spirituality.*

Point taken.

And if you don't mind, we'd kindly like to disagree with you. There are life lessons to be learned in just about everything, including movies about eccentric teenage outcasts with extraordinary perms.

We will be the first people to say that *Napoleon Dynamite* exists solely as a comedic film (okay, maybe not the *first* people, but we're definitely on the list). We can all agree the filmmakers did not set out to make some sort of grand statement about society or politics or religion. They just wanted to make us all laugh, and they did a great job.

But when some of the laughter has subsided, there are still truths to be found within the framework of the film. Why? Any good comedian will tell you that the best comedy is built on truth. Think: how many times have you heard the statement, "It's funny because it's true"?

So we laugh, not only because the movie is hilarious, but also because we recognize bits of ourselves in the characters. We empathize with Napoleon as he stands on the edges of the dance, watching everyone else participate in the fun. We feel Pedro's apprehension as he approaches the podium, skitless and, quite literally, speechless. We get angry alongside Napoleon when he tells Uncle Rico to get off his property before he calls the cops. We laugh at all these moments, but we also register with them emotionally.

So while we are laughing, we can learn something about ourselves.

Thus this book. We've attempted to reach deeper into the movie, using some of its most quotable lines and applying those themes to life in general. Some were easy; some were quite a stretch. But hopefully all of them will be applicable to you or someone you know, now or in the future. Overall, we, like much of the American public, just can't get enough of Napoleon.

So it's with this heart that we offer *Taming a Liger*. It

was really fun to work on, and we hope that shows. But more importantly, we hope the deeper truths about life and God also show through to find you wherever you are, whether you're weightless in the middle of the ocean and surrounded by tiny little sea horses or getting your head slammed against a locker. Or anywhere in between. God sees you, and we hope you'll see a bit of him as you read through this 24-piece set.

May your wildest dreams come true.

Grace and peace,
Jeff & Adam

THE 24 PIECE SET

Whatever I feel like I wanna do, gosh!

So here you are, reading this devotional about Napoleon Dynamite. Maybe it's morning and you're getting ready for school, or maybe, like Napoleon, you're on the way to somewhere. Perhaps, like Napoleon, if someone asked you what you were doing today, you'd be thrown off. Especially considering Napoleon only had one thing planned for his day: to give Mr. Action Figure a ride behind the school bus. Extremely important stuff. Besides that, his plans were probably undetermined.

Maybe you have a hot date tonight with a babe you met online, or maybe you have a dance to attend. Perhaps you have nothing to do but throw footballs at a video camera.

Whatever you've got going on, you might be even more thrown off by someone asking you what you are going to do with your life. Do you have a plan?

If you don't have a plan for your life, or even if you do, pretty much the best place to find one is in the Word. And you might be surprised that God is not necessarily asking you to create a detailed trajectory. See, for example, Micah.

Micah was a prophet at a crucial time in Israel's history. God's people had wandered far from him, worshiping other gods and following their own ways. Prophets such as Isaiah, Hosea, Amos, and Micah were sent to call the people back to the God who loved them and had their best interests in mind. Micah told the people of Israel that following their own plans could only lead to destruction. He reminded them that God has another way.

"But he's already made it plain how to live, what to do, what GOD is looking for in men and women. It's quite simple: Do what is fair and just to your neighbor, be compassionate and loyal in your love. And don't take yourself too seriously — take God seriously" (Micah 6:8).

Some will tell you that they feel a calling on their life, such as to be a teacher, a marketing guru, or a missionary.

Perhaps you feel a bit left out because you don't have such a calling on your life. When someone asks what you are going to do, you answer, "I have no idea. Gosh!" But don't worry about it. You do have a calling. It's just a little less specific than you may have expected.

For example, we are all called to be fair and just in our dealings with others. This means we don't take advantage of someone else, that we don't rip people off when selling something on eBay. Being fair involves living by a higher standard in our lives than simply "honesty is the best policy." If we are to fulfill God's call on our lives, "honesty is the *only* policy." This is living justly, and by doing so, our lives will naturally take the right form.

Another calling for each of us is to be compassionate and loyal in our love. At first this seems like an unnecessary directive, doesn't it? I mean, isn't love by definition compassionate and loyal? Perhaps. But since when did any of us live by a perfect definition? We are all prone to selfishness and being inconsiderate. We find it hard to put others — even someone we love — ahead of our own needs and interests. That is why we need to stop and remember our calling to be compassionate and loyal. To step outside nterests and focus on others.

Finally, we are called to stop taking ourselves so seriously. This does not mean that we are unimportant to God. You may have heard it said that if you were the only person on earth to have ever strayed from God, he still would have sent Jesus to suffer and die just for you. I (Jeff) believe it's true, and it can, if you let it, put to rest the thoughts that you are just a number to the Father. His love for you is what allows you to stop concentrating on yourself and begin to take God seriously. Once you know that he cares for you much better than you could care for yourself, you will be free to have more fun and stop worrying about what may come your way.

Life is meant to be lived. And you can only have a full, abundant life if you live it according to the Creator's calling.

> "But he's already made it plain how to live, what to do, what GOD is looking for in men and women. It's quite simple: Do what is fair and just to your neighbor, be compassionate and loyal in your love. And don't take yourself too seriously — take God seriously."
>
> Micah 6:8

But my lips hurt real bad!

Napoleon just wants to go home early. He's had a rough day at school already, dealing with Don's mockery and Randy's outright bullying. He just had his head banged against a locker, and he wants out.

So he calls Kip and starts trying to talk Kip into getting him out of there. Kip is obviously very busy right that second with, and this is pure conjecture, making the biggest plate of nachos ever. We all know Kip refuses to come pick him up, so Napoleon makes a desperate, last-ditch attempt to get Kip to the school, presumably to talk him into taking him home.

He has chapped lips. And they hurt real bad.

Napoleon is grasping at straws, hoping his complaining will be enough to get Kip out there. He just wants to go home.

Kip is having none of it, though, and leaves Napoleon hanging out to dry, forcing him to finish out his school day.

How do you think Napoleon feels about himself here? He's been openly mocked, bullied in front of a bunch of classmates, and rejected by his own brother. We're guessing the self-esteem meter isn't really maxed out at the moment.

Let's pretend we have a *working* time machine and that we can travel back in time. Way back in time. All the way to about 1400 BC, when the children of Israel had just escaped from their Egyptian enslavement. They were roaming around some wasteland, waiting for God to lead them into the Promised Land, their new home.

To put this into perspective, the Israelites had been under a severely oppressive regime in Egypt. They were forced into very difficult labor and generally seen as second-class citizens for the past four hundred years or so. Moses came along as God's emissary and miraculously led them out of Egypt and into the wilderness, where they were on their way to the Promised Land.

And then they started complaining. Complain, complain, complain. "We have no food." God provided food. "This food is boring; we want meat." God provided meat. Wah, wah, wah. On and on.

But my lips hurt real bad.

The Israelites spent much of their time in the wilderness grumbling and complaining, and God would have none of it. Because of their bad attitudes and lack of trust, he kept them in the wilderness for forty years before leading their descendants into the Promised Land. Turns out it was the best thing God could have done for them.

Because when it came time for them to go into the Promised Land, they discovered it was already populated, so they were forced to fight for it. They wouldn't have any room for complaining about this and that—they needed to band together and fight. By spending forty years in the wilderness, they had a desire for the land that helped them put aside their pettiness and get to the business of taking their land. Plus, they'd just spent that whole time trusting God to provide food and water for them, so God-trust was second nature to them; good thing, because they would need it.

Kip wouldn't listen to Napoleon's complaining. Unlike God, Kip couldn't see the whole picture and had no idea what his refusal would do to Napoleon.

Turns out it was the best thing Kip could have done for him.

Napoleon hangs up the phone and immediately stumbles on Principal Svadean (thank you, IMDb.com, for the character's name) trying to direct Pedro to his locker. Napoleon strikes up a conversation, shows Pedro where his locker is located, and soon finds himself at Pedro's house taking the Sledgehammer on some sweet jumps.

No complaints then. Just three feet of air. (Okay, he did hurt himself on the bike when his jump attempt snapped the board — but his complaint probably only lasted as long as his voice remained two octaves higher than usual.)

Complaining is easy to do, especially as a self-defense mechanism when your self-esteem has been wounded. Napoleon did it as a desperate attempt to get out of school (you know he was desperate because he was appealing to Kip). But complaining got Napoleon — and the Israelites — nowhere.

Imagine the self-esteem boost Napoleon got when he extended a hand of friendship to Pedro and saw that hand welcomed. Imagine the faith boost the Israelites got when they finally entered their land and started laying their enemies to waste.

Action, not complaint, is what changed their lives.

So maybe this reminder from the Israelites can help the next time you face a frustrating situation. It's tempting to complain, and there's nothing wrong with a little venting. But those complaints will do nothing to change the situation; action will. We've all heard that tired old phrase about lighting a candle instead of cursing the darkness, but even though it's been around forever, it's still true. Pray. Ask God what action you should take, if any, and then trust that he — not your tongue or bad attitude — will turn the situation around for you.

Do everything readily and cheerfully — no bickering, no second-guessing allowed!

Philippians 2:14

Dang! You got shocks

...pegs...Lucky!

Have you ever watched a small child at a friend's house, maybe while on a play date? Parents of toddlers know the behavior: the visiting child will be playing with a toy that, at that moment in time, holds a special meaning for the host child. The host child will want the toy back and give it a tug, only to hear the visiting child holler that covetous word: "Mine!"

At least kids are honest enough to *say* that sort of stuff. Admit it: the more you grow up, the less likely you are to voice your covetous thoughts. Let's imagine you're at a friend's house, enjoying some conversation over a couple of peanut butter and jelly sandwiches. And they're telling you all about the such-and-such or something-or-other they just got, and you're keeping your mouth shut, but in your heart you're screaming, "Mine!"

Unfortunately for us humans, coveting extends beyond things. Sure, you can wish you had stuff that other people have (Sledgehammer bikes, for example, perfect for sweet jumps), but coveting doesn't stop there. You can covet someone's lifestyle. You can covet someone's relationship with their mother/father/boyfriend/girlfriend/spouse/etc. You can covet someone's station in life or fancy title on their business card.

And chances are, you will. Especially if you ride the bus to school, or, even worse, are forced to suffer a trip in your Uncle Rico's bright orange van (although, most of us would agree that van's kind of cool). Napoleon thought Pedro's bike was sweet, but we know he had access to a bike all his own — we saw it when he took Kip into town for the Rex Kwon Do seminar.

So why did Napoleon think Pedro was lucky? Was he coveting the bike, or did it have more to do with wanting to escape the life he's living? Was he, in essence, coveting the lifestyle Pedro had that would allow him to have such a sweet bike?

Probably Napoleon said that about Pedro being lucky because the filmmakers thought it was a funny thing for him to say. But let's make this personal for a minute. How many times a day do you find yourself thinking, "Lucky!" about someone you know or something you heard about on the radio or saw on TV?

If you answered that last question with the word "never," then it's time to fly back to your Fortress of Solitude, Superman, and leave us regular folks alone to figure out our lives. If, on the other hand, you're a normal person, you'll identify with the problem. There's hardly a minute that goes by in our lives when we aren't being advertised to, being told we must get bigger, better, more.

Or brighter teeth.

Or softer skin.

Or safer-yet-sportier vehicles.

Or fill-in-the-blank-here.

Seems like the only message we hear anymore is that our current lives aren't good enough and that we must crave all these *things*, not for the things themselves, but because they'll make us better people.

So we look at people who get something we'd like to have

we say, "Lucky!" to them, maybe even out loud. But when we say, "Lucky!" do we really mean, "Mine!" while wishing we could grab the object out of their hands and make it our own? After all, saying, "Lucky!" to someone else indicates that maybe we don't think of ourselves as very lucky.

Of course, God has something else to say on the matter. For one thing, he mentions this inconvenient notion of being happy alongside those who have something to be happy about (see Romans 12:15). But God, as he so often does, has a way of cutting to the heart of the problem.

Jesus once taught his disciples a lesson on worry. He brought up the subject of ravens and how God feeds them, even though they don't have a nest or anything to store food in. Then Jesus pointed to some flowers and mentioned how splendidly dressed they are, even though they'll just be thrown into a fire the next day. And to drive the point home, Jesus flat-out tells the disciples not to worry because it will get them nowhere. Instead, they just need to trust God and seek his kingdom first (see Luke 12:22-31).

Worry leads to coveting. So what's the antidote? Contentment. If we can get to a point in our lives where we are legitimately content with what God has given us and trust him to continue giving us what we need — when we need it — we can overcome the part of ourselves that automatically thinks, "Lucky!" Easily said, but can it be done?

Okay, admittedly, there are no easy steps. But it boils down to letting the knowledge of God soak through from your head to your heart. You may know God will take care of you. But you must go beyond just believing it upstairs; you must let it sink in at the heart level.

Laugh with your happy friends when they're happy; share tears when they're down.

Romans 12:15

Worst day of my life, what do you think?

I (Adam) have a friend who likes to throw around the word *best*. She's always saying things like, "Oh, that is the *best* restaurant," or "I just heard the *best* song on the radio." She says it with verbal italics, an inflection on the word that lets you know how much she likes the particular item/service/ place in question. She once said, and I wish I was making this up, "*Grease II* is the *best* movie."

Obviously, when she says "best," she doesn't literally mean "better than all the rest." Her definition of "best" is skewed from the accepted definition; instead it's her particular shorthand for saying she likes something a lot.

The first day we meet him, Napoleon did have a bad day at school, but when he calls it the "worst day of [his] life," he doesn't literally mean the absolute worst day in his life; it's just his shorthand for saying he had a bad day.

We all talk like this to some extent. Saying things in extremes is just a part of our culture now, to where sentences like, "I love that shirt," or "This is the greatest banana pudding I've ever had," or "That movie was awful" are commonplace. In reality, the movie had a horrible plot, but the acting was fine and the cinematography decent. The shirt may be nice, but you aren't going to marry it. The banana pudding is tasty, but pulling up exact memories of every other banana pudding you've sampled in your lifetime is a theoretical impossibility, making that "greatest" claim a shaky one.

This extreme-speak has contributed to our overall inability to see our lives in proper perspective. So Napoleon says, "Worst day of my life," and it doesn't even throw us for a loop. We just go right along with the movie, because we've been conditioned to understand that sort of shorthand and take it for what it really means.

But consider Job. Way back in the Old Testament days

(scholars estimate around 1200 years before Christ), there lived a guy named Job. Job was a wealthy guy, but keep in mind that wealth in those days was measured more in the amount of livestock and land you had than in actual money. Job's story is interesting, because he had a day where he had every reason to say, "Worst day of my life." In *one day*, Job incurred the following losses:

- ⊙ All his oxen and donkeys were stolen by the Sabeans, who killed the servants Job had hired to tend the flocks.
- ⊙ All his sheep and the servants tending them were struck by lightning and killed.
- ⊙ All his camels were stolen by the Chaldeans, who also killed the servants in charge of them.
- ⊙ All his sons and daughters were killed when a tornado caused their house to collapse on them.

Worst day of his life? Yeah, that qualifies.

So Job had just lost his wealth and his children, no doubt whom he loved. And what did he say? "God gave it all and God can take it all away. May his name be praised" (Job 1:13-21). The book goes on for forty-one more chapters, consisting mostly of Job sticking to that perspective despite outside pressure from his wife and friends.

About 1300 years later, another guy came along and said basically the same thing. Peter, one of Jesus' disciples, wrote a letter to the early church and encouraged them to give their anxieties and worries to God, because God cares for them (see 1 Peter 5:7).

Everyone — you and me included — has problems, and sometimes those problems can overwhelm us and cause us to think we're having the worst day of our lives. Sometimes those problems are so bad that the statement becomes true and we really do find a new winner of the Worst Day of My Life Award.

Even so, God said those problems aren't supposed to be ours.

They belong to him.

He wants them, because he knows we'll just buckle under the burden. No matter how much you work out, you'll never be buff enough to carry that stuff around. Let God take it for you.

eally wants it. He said so.

ifficult to maintain the proper perspective on

your life when you're being crushed by a weight you aren't qualified — or meant — to carry. Giving God the load gives you the freedom to look at life as it really is. Pretty sweet.

GOD gives, GOD takes.
God's name be ever blessed.

Job 1:21

5

I said come down here and see what happens when you try to hit me!

I think we all know what happened when Napoleon tried to hit Kip. We saw that Kip does, in fact, have the worst reflexes of all time.

Just what is a cage fighter anyway? And why does Kip think he can become one?

Kip would probably say he is pursuing his dreams, while most of us would say he is living in a dream world — and needs to wake up now.

Kip's idea of himself is very different from how we view him. Perception is seriously a big deal.

Have you ever listened to your voice as it was recorded, say on a voice recorder or even on videotape? You probably said something like, "That doesn't sound like me!" And you would be right — sort of. When you speak out loud, your jawbone vibrates your eardrum, sending signals to your brain. This is how you "hear" yourself. Your friends, however, hear your voice from the sound waves that travel through the air to their eardrums. Thus, how you are heard by a person standing next to you is different from how you hear yourself. So which of these is your "real" voice — the one you hear or the one your friends hear?

The answer, of course, is both. Yet because we use our voice primarily to communicate with others (unless you really like talking to yourself), we work to make our "outer" voice the best it can be so we can be properly understood.

In the same way, we have two ways of being seen. There is the way we perceive ourselves, what we consider ourselves to be. And there is the way others perceive us, what they consider us to be. And they are different, just as our two voices are different.

You may see yourself as an introvert, not a "people person" or very good in public settings. Yet others sense a real depth about you and like being around you. They come away feeling better about themselves from spending time with you.

Or perhaps you envision yourself as overly cautious,

afraid of taking risks. Others see you, however, as a person of great wisdom, carefully considering the options before making the right decision.

Both how you see yourself and how others perceive you are legitimate viewpoints. But there is another point of view that is even more legitimate and much more important. That is how God sees you.

How do you think God sees you? When he gazes at you intently, what does he see? This is a vitally important question to answer, as it will shape how you see yourself and how others see you. It will also determine the path you take for all of eternity.

Once in a while (and sometimes a lot), we miss the mark God has set for us. We all sin, but because of Christ, even our offenses against God don't get in the way of his perspective on who we are. He no longer looks at you as one who has broken his rules and by doing so became a broken person. God calls us "saints" (see Romans 1:7, NIV). He says we are already citizens of heaven (see Philippians 3:20). And here is what Paul writes to the church at Corinth. (If you know the history of this church, you know they had nothing to brag about on their own.)

One man died for everyone. That puts everyone in the same boat.

He included everyone in his death so that everyone could also be included in his life, a resurrection life, a far better life than people ever lived on their own.

Because of this decision we don't evaluate people by what they have or how they look. We looked at the Messiah that way once and got it all wrong, as you know. We certainly don't look at him that way anymore. Now we look inside, and what we see is that anyone united with the Messiah gets a fresh start, is created new. The old life is gone; a new life burgeons! Look at it! All this comes from the God who settled the relationship between us and him, and then called us to settle our relationships with each other. God put the world square with himself through the Messiah, giving the world a fresh start by offering forgiveness of sins. (2 Corinthians 5:14-19)

Wow! How great is this?! We no longer look at others, or ourselves, like we used to. We don't have to judge — or be judged — by our appearance or by what we own. Our identity — to ourselves, to others, and to God — is based on what Jesus has already done for us.

This is reality. It does not matter what our reflexes are like; God sees us all as cage fighters now.

> *Because of this decision we don't evaluate people by what they have or how they look. . . . Now we look inside, and what we see is that anyone united with the Messiah gets a fresh start, is created new.*
>
> 2 Corinthians 5:16-17

Maybe you'd be interested in some home-woven handicrafts.

Have you ever done something so many times you feel like you can do it in your sleep? I (Adam) used to write on-hold messages for a living — very formulaic advertisements that play over phone systems. After three years of doing it, I was able to carry on a conversation with someone while writing an on-hold message. That's how boringly easy the task had become. I was, in a sense, making an infinity of home-woven handicrafts.

Sound familiar? We all have things that we do so much they become a drudgery to us. There's no telling how many hours Deb must've put into weaving those boondoggle keychains, but the end goal of earning money to go to college made it worth her while.

There is a time, usually more than once, in everyone's life when something becomes a dirge of repetition. It may be on the job, it may be at home, it may be at church. And there's a dividing line between the things we must do and the things we only do out of convenience or because the idea of changing our routine is scary. For Deb, it was the former. She was driven to make all those keychains and then attempt to sell them because her focus wasn't on weaving plastic thread into a fashionable way to tote keys; she was focused on taking the next step in her education. The keychains, and her Glamour Shots business, were merely ways to propel her onto that step.

So maybe it's time for you to take a long, hard look at your life and determine the areas where you're making home-woven handicrafts. And then determine why. Are you just working that routine job because you're comfortable there, or is it because you're using it as a stepping-stone toward a greater end goal? If it's the latter, you understand the drive that comes with having an end in mind.

It's called hope.

If you don't have a driving purpose, like Deb's desire to go to college, then the task becomes unbearable and pointless. But no matter what our jobs, we aren't meant to work only for the sake of the job. God wants us to have a higher purpose to our work; he wants us to view our time here on earth through the lens of eternity. And sometimes that means weaving, weaving, and more weaving.

You may have done something a million times, but that doesn't mean you're done with it. God may have something in store for you on the million-and-first time that completely changes your life. You just can't see the whole picture as God sees it. King Solomon, the wisest man ever to walk the earth, touched on this as he mused about work and the seeming pointlessness it can sometimes have. He said that God made the world to be beautiful to us, yet in a way that never fully satisfies us. Why? Because we were made for eternity.

So God made us to thrive in eternity, but we're here in this finite world, incapable of seeing the complete picture God sees. What can we do? We do the task he's set in front of us, regardless of how many times we've already done it. And we do it because that task isn't the point of our lives — the hope of eternity is.

Years upon years after Solomon wrote his musings about eternity, a man was hanging out by the pool. Not a swimming pool, a special pool that supposedly had the power to heal people. Every now and then the water of the pool would stir, and, according to some biblical manuscripts, the first person in the water at that point would be miraculously healed.

So there was this disabled man lying beside the pool. He'd been an invalid thirty-eight years, and a lot of those years had been spent poolside. But he was never able to get in because, as you can imagine, there was quite the crowd of diseased people constantly waiting there. The waters would stir and someone else would get in before he was able to.

What kept that guy hanging at the pool? Why did he wait there, day after day after day? The hope of healing. The hope that his life could mean something more if he just stuck with this particular task of waiting. The hope that things would change through his consistency. He believed.

And then along comes Jesus. And Jesus asks the man if he wants to get better. And the man has the hope of healing. And Jesus heals him on the spot.

Consistent hope.

It keeps your eyes focused on the right thing, ultimately.

Have an eternal mindset so you can get glimpses of things the way God intended. And when you're stuck making an infinity of boondoggle keychains, take your eyes off the boondoggle and set them on infinity itself.

God can do anything, you know — far more than you could ever imagine or guess or request in your wildest dreams! He does it not by pushing us around but by working within us, his Spirit deeply and gently within us.

Ephesians 3:20

So me and you are pretty much friends now, right?

So you've got my back and everything?

Having a friend to watch your back is a pretty good idea. Napoleon had Pedro's back, first by helping him get a wig to cover his shaved head, then to win election as class president with his awesome dance. And Pedro had Napoleon's back, telling him which skill he should use to get a babe to go to the dance with him.

Who has your back?

Sometimes we think we don't need any help, that we have everything under control. David, king of Israel, was a mighty warrior. He had killed Goliath, the giant, and thus earned the nickname "Giant Killer." He led many men into battle and always came away the winner. David needed someone to watch his back? Hardly.

Until the day that the Philistines — the perennial enemy of Israel — picked a fight with David and his men. And, once again, David led the charge. One of the Philistines was a descendant of the giants named Ishbi-Benob, and he went straight for David. This giant had a spear that weighed eight pounds and a brand-new suit of armor. He announced to all who would listen that he intended to kill the Giant Killer.

David and Ishbi-Benob squared off. A battle raged all around, but for now it was just the two of them, the giant and the Giant Killer. They fought furiously, but unlike when he fought Goliath, David could not gain the edge he needed to put this giant away. And after a while, David began to move a bit slower. His muscles ached and his vision blurred. He was exhausted, and Ishbi-Benob knew it. The giant moved in for the kill. He would be the greatest warrior in the world, the man who killed the Giant Killer.

But David did have someone watching his back. Abishai came to his rescue, struck Ishbi-Benob dead, and saved

David's life. (Not as cool as a dance in front o
school, but no less brave.)

Who has your back?

Faith is not meant to be lived out alone. God has designed us to do life together. The smallest group Jesus ever sent out on a mission was two—he never sent his followers out alone. Why? Because he knows that we do not function well alone. We need companionship, we need encouragement, we need accountability.

We need someone to watch our back.

Where can you find a friend who will be there when you become too exhausted to fight the enemy? Typically, you find each other through mutual interests or a situation you both find yourselves in. Napoleon and Pedro were both outcasts in their school. While everyone else was on the track or on the field with their friends, goofing off and doing a few exercises, Napoleon and Pedro stayed in the bleachers, unwanted by anyone else. This is how they found themselves together. They didn't plan it or go looking for each other—they were just there. Perhaps you are in a situation like that: a small group, a class, a division in your company where you and one other person seem to gravitate together by default.

Or maybe you have become friends through other similarities. You have children the same age. You both like to fish. You have a horse and he has a saddle. It doesn't matter how you come together, you need someone in your life to watch your back. Someone to hold you accountable.

That's straight from the Bible, not just some philosophical rhetoric.

"Make this your common practice: Confess your sins to each other and pray for each other so that you can live together whole and healed" (James 5:16).

"Therefore encourage one another and build up each other, as indeed you are doing" (1 Thessalonians 5:11, NRSV).

"Friends love through all kinds of weather" (Proverbs 17:17).

If you can bear to take your beloved *Napoleon Dynamite* DVD out of the player for just a while, watch (or watch again) *The Return of the King*, the final installment in the masterful storytelling of J. R. R. Tolkien's classic series. It is worth watching all three films, nearly ten hours worth of cinema, just for a ten-second scene. Frodo and Sam are climbing Mount Doom to reach the pit where Frodo must cast the ring. They are almost to their destination when Frodo, exhausted and spent physically, emotionally, and spiritually, falls to the ground, unable to move at all. In one of the greatest acts of selflessness and love, Sam scoops up Frodo in his arms and says,

"I cannot carry your burden for you, Mr. Frodo. But I can carry you." And he does just that, carrying Frodo the rest of the way.

Do you have a friend like Sam who will pick you up and carry you when you can go no farther? Do you have someone like Napoleon who, at the risk of shaming himself in front of the entire school, will put on an impromptu skit to help you win the election? Do you have someone to walk your faith journey with you and hold you accountable for your growth? Who has your back?

So speak encouraging words to one another. Build up hope so you'll all be together in this, no one left out, no one left behind.

1 Thessalonians 5:11

You gonna eat your tots?
Can I have 'em?

There they sat. Stacked neatly, a perfect potato pyramid, resting atop a field of Styrofoam. So tantalizing. So delicious. So greasy.

The tots.

Pedro is apparently not a tot-lover. Napoleon, as we know, is. He (Napoleon) eyes them across the table. Already finished with his own, he sees them on Pedro's tray, untouched and looking oh-so-tasty. Either Pedro is saving them, in order to savor their wonderful flavor as the final part of his meal, or he doesn't like them. The suspense is unbearable, and Napoleon finally dares to venture forth a question.

"You gonna eat your tots?"

57

Negative, comes the reply. The first stage in the Great Tot Caper complete, Napoleon takes the next tentative step.

"Can I have 'em?"

A nod from Pedro. "Sure."

Yesssssss.

Put yourself in this scene. You're Pedro and a friend or relative or acquaintance or just some random dude/girl is asking for your tots.

What would you do?

What *should* you do?

What should you do when your baby has grown out of her newborn clothes, and there's a soon-to-be single mother in your church?

What should you do when you're finished with a book everyone needs to read for class, and a classmate can't afford to buy it?

What should you do when your coworker forgot his lunch, and you have an extra five-dollar bill in your pocket?

These questions tend to answer themselves: You give 'em your tots.

Kids are taught from about age zero that they're supposed to share. It's a message that gets hammered in at an early age. So why do we have so much trouble remembering it when we grow up? At what point in our development do we become selfish to the point of holding back tots that we won't eat? Some of us even wonder why we should give of ourselves at all.

Jesus had a little something to say about it. He once talked about money — stuff — and the proper outlook toward it. Basically, it boils down to your heart attitude and whether you're willing to let your stuff go or if you'd rather hoard it and hang on to it and refuse to let it out of your sight.

But Jesus puts it plain and simple. He says that if you're trustworthy with a little bit, then God will trust you with more. But if you hang on to a little bit, that's all you're going to get (see Luke 16:10-13).

An example: Napoleon stuffs the tots in his pocket. One even falls onto the bench and instead of letting it go, Napoleon grabs that tot and wedges it in with all its potato brethren.

Along comes class and Napoleon gets a jones for some tots (really, who among us hasn't at some time in our lives?). He unzips the pocket, takes a bite from one tot, and is immediately accosted by Randy, the school bully, demanding some of Napoleon's tots.

Faced with this situation, I wouldn't have given Randy the tots, either. He's a bully and he doesn't deserve them, especially since he didn't ask. But I think it's interesting that Napoleon hoards the tots, refuses to give them up (and even lies by saying he's "friggin' starving and hasn't eaten all day"), and then — he loses them all when Randy kicks the pocket, mushes the bounty of tot goodness, and makes them too gross to eat.

Try to hang on to your stuff; watch it get smashed in your pocket.

If you hang on to a little bit of stuff, that's all you're going to get.

So here's a question for you: What if someone asks for your tots and you really *are* going to eat them? What do you do then? What if it's someone you don't like, probably how Napoleon felt about Randy? It's a judgment call for you, really. Perhaps it will make the decision easier when you remember what Jesus said about those who are trustworthy with their stuff — it's a great way to get more stuff.

Look at it this way — if you close your metaphorical hand

around your metaphorical stuff, there's no way that get replaced with something better. Keep your hand open and there's no telling what great thing God will put there.

Now, that analogy has been misused often in the church world to mean that you need to put more money in the offering bucket. But that misuse doesn't make it any less true — God looks at your heart, and if you have an open-handed attitude (or open-pocketed, in Napoleon's case), he'll make sure to provide for you. Develop a sharing heart and watch God share his all with you.

Jesus went on to make these comments:
If you're honest in small things,
you'll be honest in big things;
If you're a crook in small things,
you'll be a crook in big things.
If you're not honest in small jobs,
who will put you in charge of the store?

Luke 16:10-12

You could be drinking whole if you wanted to.

What a way to start a conversation. "I see you're drinking 1 percent. Is that 'cause you think you're fat? 'Cause you're not. You could be drinking whole if you wanted to."

Seriously, Napoleon. What were you thinking? I mean, I know you're all tongue-tied talking to the pretty girl and all, but . . . seriously. That's the best you can come up with? Come on, man.

But, the thing is . . . he was telling the truth.

And he was so "Napoleon" about it.

Can you imagine Napoleon sitting down at Deb's table and opening up with a line like, "So, peanut butter and jelly — it's not tots, but it'll do," or "I haven't seen you

63

around school before; you new here?" or the worst, "Hey, Sweetheart, my name's Napoleon. What'd you say we go out on Friday?"

Not exactly Napoleon style.

Instead, Napoleon was just who he was: clumsy, maladjusted, off-beat Napoleon Dynamite, the character we know and love. He meant no ill intent; rather, he was trying to be nice. He was abrupt and blunt, but that's only because he has no tact in the first place. The point is, his heart was in the right place, and though the words weren't exactly the smoothest they could be, they did the trick and opened the door to a friendship with Deb.

Napoleon spoke the truth, and he did it in love.

There's a multifaceted word: "Love." It has many connotations, but here we aren't talking about it in the romantic sense but in the "love of our fellow human beings" sense. Napoleon wasn't trying to harm Deb, he was trying to pay her a compliment; it just came out wrong. But I think Deb saw the attitude behind it and knew Napoleon wasn't being mean. His heart was in the right place, in a place of love, of caring about her feelings, something he isn't ordinarily very good at.

Back in the times of the early church, the apostle Paul wrote a lot of letters to different churches as a means of keeping everyone on the same page. Many of those letters contribute to the New Testament, and one of them was written to a church in Ephesus.

Here's something to understand about Paul. He was quite Napoleon-like in his ability to be blunt, and many times in his letters he would openly rebuke churches for doing things that were ungodly. He pulled no punches; instead, he knew that honest, open truth was what they needed to hear, as long as they knew he was saying it not as a way of tearing them down but as a way of building them up.

He even addressed this in his letter to the church at Ephesus. He was going on in this long passage, telling them all about building unity within their church members and how we all have different personalities and tasks God wants us to perform. And then he caps it all off by telling them that to keep themselves from listening to all the little lying voices that would try to lead them astray, they need to talk to each other truthfully, but lovingly (see Ephesians 4:15).

Speak the truth, but do it in love.

You aren't fat, so drink the milk you want to drink.

So how are you when it comes to telling people the truth about themselves? Do you hold back what you know to be true? Do you offer the truth, but do it in a destructive way in order to build yourself up or make yourself look better?

Imagine if Napoleon hadn't said anything to Deb other than "I have your stuff in my locker." No mention of her appearance. Deb is obviously nervous having Napoleon at the table, and she now has no reassurance of what he thinks of her, because he isn't saying anything; he's hiding his true thoughts and feelings for no real reason. There's no telling where their relationship would head at that point.

Or let's say Napoleon sits down and says, "I see you're drinking 1 percent. Good thing—you don't want to get fat." He's essentially still saying that Deb isn't "fat." But it's a good thing he avoids that phrasing; his way is much more kind. In my imagined version, he spoke the truth, he said almost the same thing, but subtly implied that Deb isn't desirable to Napoleon if she did get fat. I'm pretty sure Napoleon doesn't want to imply *that*.

What do you do with the truth? Do you speak it ʼngly? Do you speak it at all? We only get one shot at ʼfe; let us not waste our time holding back truths that can help people. Instead, let us speak the truth — and only the truth — and let's do it with a loving heart. We may not always get the words right, but the attitude will be there, and the world will see it.

We will be drinking whole.

God wants us to grow up, to know the whole truth and tell it in love — like Christ in everything. We take our lead from Christ, who is the source of everything we do.

Ephesians 4:15

You ever come across anything like time travel?

Where would you go if you could travel back in time? What special moment would you want to relive? Or do you want to undo a part of your past in order to have a different life now?

Time travel presents a number of paradoxes involving changing the past and its impact on the present. For instance, if you were to go back in time and convince your mother to hook up with someone besides your dad, that would mean you would not be born. Yet if you were never born, you would not have traveled back in time to sway your mother, which means she still would have been with your dad, and you would be born, meaning . . .

It gets pretty confusing. So let's say Uncle Rico did go back to 1982 and relive the state championship football game, how might that change his life? And how would those changes affect the past? And how would that past change other things about the present? This is getting really confusing.

You may be curious, like Uncle Rico, about how a person could actually time travel? First you would need to find a way to travel at a speed close to the speed of light. As you approach light speed, time slows down, and when you reach light speed, time stops still. So how can you go faster when time has no direction? The answer involves physics and something called "quantum tunneling," though suffice it to say it is theoretically possible. Once you find your quantum tunnel and begin moving faster than light, time moves backward and before you know it, it's 1982 and you're leading your team to the state championship.

The two most frightening times for most of us are the present and the future. The past, though we may have regrets or hurts, is at least familiar to us. It is the unknown about today and tomorrow that scares us.

What we are looking for is something to hold onto that will not move in the storminess of the future. Something that will stay the same as everything around us changes.

Fortunately, Jesus is just the anchor we are looking for.

Things were not easy for those who followed Jesus in the decades immediately after his death and resurrection. Christians were hounded, persecuted, imprisoned, even killed for their faith. Things were not good today, and tomorrow looked worse. This was the condition for the early Christians who read a letter, anonymously written, that circulated throughout the churches in the first century. The writer addresses situations within and without the church that these Christians faced.

⊙ Remember to show love to all, especially strangers.

⊙ Take care of those in prison, as if you were in their shoes.

⊙ In a similar way, take care of those who are tortured for their faith.

⊙ Honor and protect the sanctity of marriage.

⊙ Don't get wrapped up in material things or the pursuit of money.

⊙ Don't be misled by false teaching, especially that which loads you down with lots of rules and regulations. Let your heart be strengthened by grace.

In other words, the present is tough, and the future doesn't look too bright, either. Yet in the middle of these exhortations, the writer of the book of Hebrews makes this incredible statement:

"Jesus Christ is the same yesterday and today and forever" (Hebrews 13:8, NRSV).

Jesus does not change. We can buy a time machine on the Internet, put in the crystals and go backward to any year you can imagine, and Jesus will still be the Son of God, offering forgiveness of sin and reconciliation with the Father. We can put the T-bar between our legs, have Kip turn on the power and go forward in time as far as we can imagine and Jesus will still be there, not changing, giving life through grace and not rules.

David, the great king of Israel, wrote a song with these lyrics.

> Is there anyplace I can go to avoid your
> Spirit? To be out of your sight? If I climb to
> the sky, you're there! If I go underground,
> you're there! If I flew on morning's wings,
> to the far western horizon, you'd find me

in a minute — you're already there waiting!
Then I said to myself, 'Oh, he even sees me
in the dark! At night I'm immersed in the
light!' It's a fact: darkness isn't dark to you;
night and day, darkness and light, they're
all the same to you. (Psalm 139:7-12)

Wow. Can we assume that we cannot outrun God
even through time travel? That God is present in the past
and in the future, just as he is in the now? The answer is a
loud YES — God is everywhere, at all times. He does not
change — ever. And the best time to talk with him is always
right now.

Right on. Right on.

For Jesus doesn't change — yesterday, today, tomorrow, he's always totally himself.

Hebrews 13:8

11

It's pretty much my favorite animal.

Sitting on the front steps of the school, Napoleon sketches a liger. Part lion, part tiger, bred for its skills in magic. This, as we already know, is perfectly normal behavior for Napoleon.

One of the things I (Adam) like about Napoleon is his willingness to accept the abnormal realm. He draws the liger, yes, but he also draws a winged unicorn, a barbaric warrior holding a many-bladed axe (see the opening credits), a mace-wielding female centaur (again, opening credits), and Pedro riding atop a dragon with bloody antennae.

All played for humor, yes, but all creative, in their own unique way.

Why do we laugh when Napoleon begins to talk about the Loch Ness Monster as a current event? What is funny about summoning local wizards to protect Nessie, our underwater ally?

What is so dang funny about the supernatural?

In *Napoleon Dynamite*, the supernatural is portrayed for laughs. In any random horror movie opening this weekend at your local theater, the supernatural is portrayed for fright. Very seldom is the supernatural portrayed as pleasant or true, and if it is, it's highly unlikely that it'll be portrayed as being from God.

Yet God is a supernatural God.

Being supernatural is just plain natural for him.

Want proof? He created the world, for starters. Just because he wanted to. He didn't create ligers, no, but he did create the lion and the tiger, both of which are a marvel of craftsmanship. The same mind that dreamed up those beasts dreamt up sea snakes and pink flamingos and dung beetles; willow trees and sunflowers; the Marianas Trench and cirrus clouds and Pikes Peak.

There's a wonderful passage toward the end of the book of Job (chapters 38-41) where God very matter-of-factly (with a hint of sarcasm, even) tells Job and the assembled audience what creation was like. It's much too detailed to discuss in-depth here, but I highly recommend you read it to get a snapshot of God's immense super-nature.

Then look at Jesus. He performed his first recorded miracle to keep a party from fizzling out. Jesus, and his disciples, and his mother Mary, were at a wedding party when the hosts ran out of wine. Mary makes him aware of the problem and he remedies it with a quick miracle, changing barrels of water into the desired beverage. And not cheap wine, either — the banquet master said it was the best wine that night (see John 2:1-11).

Or take his miraculous feeding of the five thousand. You've heard the story, I'm sure. Jesus is preaching to a large crowd when they all realize they're hungry. And no one has any food. Now, I wouldn't classify this as an urgent situation needing the immediate attention of Almighty God. It's just a bunch of hungry people who didn't plan ahead. No one's about to die of starvation; they aren't on the brink of destruction.

So what? Jesus has compassion on the people. He gets five loaves of bread and a couple of fish, blesses them, thanks God for them, and has the disciples pass them around. A little while later, everyone's tummy is full and there are twelve baskets of food left over (see Mark 6:30-42). It wasn't Jesus showing off; it was Jesus being who he was, and still is.

Supernatural.

We've heard these stories for so long that we've forgotten who they're really about. We've forgotten that God specifically told us that he never changes (see Hebrews 13:8). He was supernatural then, so he's supernatural now. But as a culture, we're so jaded and cynical about it that we scoff at the very idea. We'd rather laugh at ligers, thank you very much.

But here's the thing. I'm writing this in a standard word-processing program that normally tells me with a red squiggly line when I've misspelled a word. And there's no squiggly line under the word "liger."

It's a real word. Because a liger is a real animal, a cross between a male lion and a female tiger (seriously, there really is such a thing — do a Google search and you'll find it). There's also a "tigon," a cross between a male tiger and a female lion. These animals usually exist because of human influence, but they exist nonetheless. They aren't bred in real life for their skills in magic, but they are here.

The supernatural exists because God exists.

Let us not lose our sense of the wonder of this world. Let us not forget that the God who created it, who did all the things recorded in the Bible, longs for our companionship.

Let us not turn a cold shoulder to the God of the miraculous, capable of doing all things. Let us approach him with awe and reverence. For he is great, and greatly to be praised.

> *"Can you get the attention of the clouds, and commission a shower of rain? Can you take charge of the lightning bolts and have them report to you for orders?"*
>
> Job 38:34-35

We need some way to make us look official — like we've got all the answers.

I (Jeff) have heard that in real estate, the three most important things when selling a property are location, location, and location. In our real lives, when it comes to selling ourselves, the three most important things are appearance, appearance, appearance.

Or so it seems.

To appear official, Kip suggested he and Uncle Rico wear jewelry, while Rico felt name tags were the way to go. But, as we all know, just because they wore name tags didn't mean they were official — but the name tags served to cover their lack of experience.

Often, we do a similar thing. We try to manipulate our

appearance so we look like the person we want to be. Here are some of my thoughts on how we try to disguise ourselves:

- ⊙ We dress in the latest fashion fad (even if that fad lasts only about a week).
- ⊙ We adopt different hairstyles, colors, shapes, and lengths (maybe even a medieval warrior-looking wig).
- ⊙ We hang around the "cool" or popular crowd, which gives us the appearance of being cool by osmosis. Or, we hang around the "geek" crowd so we can appear like we don't care.
- ⊙ We talk about the newest "hip" movies, music, or books, whether we really like them or not.
- ⊙ Or, we even carry around a tattered Bible or classic piece of literature to make us look super spiritual and/or super smart.

All of these methods, and others, are meant to give the impression we are someone we are not. We desperately want to look official, like we have all the answers. And for a while, maybe, we can get away with it. Others take us for who we want to be, not who we are. After a while, we can even convince ourselves that this is the "real me." But God is not impressed with any show we put on.

Case in point: King Saul. He was taller than the average man by a head, and very handsome. He just had that "look" a king should have. But then he stepped outside of the boundaries God had set for him, and his disobedience cost him and the people he ruled greatly. God sent Samuel, a prophet and judge in Israel, to search for a new king who would follow God's orders.

Samuel went to see Jesse, a good man who had good-looking sons. Samuel saw the eldest son, Eliab, and thought, *wow — he looks like what a king should look like. He has the walk and the talk. I'm sure this is the one God sent me to choose for Israel's next leader.* But God held Samuel back from anointing Eliab king. "I don't look on the outer person," said God. "I look on the heart. This one is not the one I have chosen."

So Samuel asked Jesse to bring forth his next son. Once again, Samuel looked at the boy and thought, *He looks like a king.* Yet God said again, "This is not the one. He may look kingly to you, but I see all the way through to the heart."

This happened seven times, with Jesse's seven oldest

sons. Finally, Samuel said, “Is this it, or do you have another?”

“There is one more,” said Jesse, “though I doubt you’d be interested in him. He’s the youngest — the runt of the pack.”

“Send for him anyway,” said Samuel.

So the youngest son of Jesse was sent for. When he arrived, Samuel agreed with Jesse. This one was a runt. He was way too young to be a king — and he smelled like sheep. But God told Samuel, “This is the one I have chosen. Anoint him king.” So Samuel did, then rode back home, while David stayed with his brothers, filled inside with the Spirit of God.

While people look on the outside, God looks on the inside where the real person lives.

Sometime later while Saul was still king, the Israelites were faced with an overwhelming enemy army, led by a giant of a man named Goliath. David, on an errand to deliver food to his brothers in Saul’s army, volunteered to fight Goliath one-on-one. Saul found a suit of armor and a ord for David to use. Once he put this on, however, ld hardly move.

"This is not the person I am," he said. shepherd. Let me be who I really am."

Saul agreed, and David went out dressed humbly, carrying only a slingshot. The rest, of course, you know. David killed the giant Goliath with one shot and later was king over Israel.

Putting on an "official" name tag did not make Kip a salesman. He proved that by backing over a NuPont fiber-woven bowl with Rico's van, bursting it to pieces. Putting on clothing or getting a new hairstyle or hanging with cool people cannot change who you really are. God sees through everything on the outside and looks at your heart. Even Glamour Shots by Deb cannot hide your heart from God. Just be who you are.

> But GOD told Samuel, "Looks aren't everything. Don't be impressed with his looks and stature . . . GOD judges persons differently than humans do. Men and women look at the face; GOD looks into the heart."
>
> 1 Samuel 16:7

You know, like bow-hunting skills, nunchuck skills, computer-hacking skills. Girls only want boyfriends who have great skills!

Deb said yes . . . to Pedro.

And it was killing Napoleon.

He was already upset about Pedro asking Deb to the dance, since she's pretty much the only girl in school he's interested in. Besides, Napoleon had already helped Pedro in his extravagant cake-building gesture to ask Summer to the dance. Sure, she'd said no, but Pedro didn't know that before he'd asked Deb to the dance, too.

And she said yes.

Napoleon's opinion of himself must've been shattered.

The only girl in school that he could possibly have a chance of taking to the dance (let's face it — Trisha was most certainly *not* a willing companion), and she was going with Pedro. At the moment he and Pedro unfolded Deb's positive note, Napoleon lost all hope of going to the dance with someone, and he says as much.

"Well nobody's going to go out with me!"

Not really splitting hairs there, is he? No hidden subtext in that statement. He's despondent, and he's readily admitting it.

But what he says next is fascinating (and funny). He offers his reasoning on why he thinks no one will go out with him: "I don't even have any good skills. You know, like numchuk skills, bow-hunting skills, computer-hacking skills. Girls only want boyfriends who have great skills!"

Setting aside Napoleon's assertions about the fairer gender, let's take a look at the underlying thought here. Napoleon's essentially saying that he doesn't have anything to offer a girl, and will therefore be lonely and without a girlfriend.

Napoleon feels like he doesn't matter.

And while we understand why he would feel that way, feeling somewhat rejected — God says, as a matter of fact, he does matter.

Jesus said it too. Talking about how God takes care of his people, he mentions how much people count in God's eyes (see Luke 12:24). Thousands of years earlier, Moses wrote about the way God blesses his people and makes them the head and not the tail (see Deuteronomy 28:13).

God cares about people.

God values people.

Don't believe it? The most conclusive proof is in the gospel of John, where Jesus flat-out says that God loved people so much that he sent Jesus into the world to save them (see John 3:16).

Value.

Napoleon wasn't feeling valued at the moment, but the value was still there.

His self-esteem had taken so much of a beating that he didn't even realize that his own experience contradicted his statement about not having any skills. While "drawing" isn't necessarily the most action-packed skill (not action-packed enough to make Napoleon's list of essential girl-impressing skills), it is a skill nonetheless, and a skill Napoleon, to some degree, possesses.

Which Pedro points out, nonchalantly.

It's imperceptible, but Napoleon's scrawny chest swells with the realization that yes, he is good at drawing, like, animals and warriors and stuff. In fact, he's probably the best that he knows of.

We all have something that we're good at; God set it up that way. We also all have things we're not so good at. Again, it's just the way things are set up. A key to feeling good about yourself is to focus on the things you're good at and realize that there are things you aren't going to be so good at.

Napoleon isn't the best artist in the world, but he knows what he likes, and he knows his way around the pencil and paper well enough to be dangerous with it. His picture of Trisha is certainly better than I can do. I (Adam) get the feeling Napoleon finished that drawing, sat back, admired it, and felt pretty darn good about himself.

He finally saw his value, though it had been there all along. (And when Trisha said yes, regardless of her motivation, Napoleon felt elated. "My woman I'm taking to the dance" is a pretty confident statement, if you ask me.)

You have value, though you may not see it.

There will be times in life when you find it difficult to

see that value. Sometimes it gets so difficult to see that you forget it's even there at all.

But it's still there.

No matter how cloudy or stormy or rainy it gets outside, the sun never stops shining. It's always there, bringing heat to the planet, though you may not see or feel it.

Napoleon realized his value and put it to work. And it started a chain reaction of confidence in him that eventually led to his phenomenal dance moves debut for all his classmates to see.

If you can't see your value, look for it. Pray that God would reveal it to you through his Word. Seek him and he will guide you to the place where you realize who you are and what he made you to be.

Look at the ravens, free and unfettered, not tied down to a job description, carefree in the care of God. And you count far more.

Luke 12:24

Took me like three hours to finish the shading on your upper lip. It's probably the best drawing I've ever done.

One remarkable thing about Napoleon is that he goes all out in everything he does. If he's going to do something, he's going to *do* it. He's determined to throw that action figure out the bus window, and no threat of the bus driver seeing it will stop him. He's determined to talk about the Loch Ness Monster as a "current event," and no amount of snickering from the class will stop him. He's determined to get to the school dance on time, and no amount of dirt road will stop him.

He's determined to draw a picture of Trisha Stevens, and no lack of actual artistic talent will stop him.

There is not enough of this kind of determination in the world today.

We are much too willing to give up.

Things get difficult or look like they'll take awhile, and suddenly we lose interest in what we were just gung-ho about. I (Adam) remember when I was young, I wanted to learn how to play guitar. My brother was learning, so I figured I could just use his guitar and lesson book and I'd learn that way. Piece of cake.

And then I tried to play the thing. I pressed down on the strings, attempting to make chords like the book showed me, but when I strummed, it sounded bad because I wasn't pressing hard enough. So I pressed harder and got the right sound, but I also got a whole lot of pain in my fingertips.

Turns out that playing guitar hurts. All guitar players will tell you it takes time to get your fingers properly calloused. Eventually they will have the toughness of medieval warriors, but until then, you'd better be prepared to deal with some pain.

I was not. I learned two chords, played for a total of maybe twenty minutes, and decided I was done. Suddenly the guitar lost its appeal. I tried to pick it up again a couple of years later and had the same result. The pain in my fingers was too great to bear, so I said, "Forget this," and went outside to practice jumping my bike on driveway curbs.

Finally, the third time was the charm. I picked it up, fought through the pain, and have had my guitar-calloused fingertips for the past thirteen years, several of which I spent earning a living playing, you guessed it, guitar.

It took time, effort, and the sacrifice of my personal finger comfort, but it was worth it. The guitar was my "shading on the upper lip."

What's yours?

Another story: King David was Israel's greatest king, but he was on his deathbed. For the longest time, he had wanted to build a temple, a permanent home for God, but because of war and unrest in the kingdom, he was never able to achieve this goal. Instead, the task fell to David's son, Solomon.

Once Solomon's throne was established, he set about making his father's dream come true; he started to build a temple. Here's a sampling of what he did:

- ⊙ He contacted a neighboring king to ask for the best in materials and labor that the king had to offer.
- ⊙ He conscripted tens of thousands of people from Israel, the best craftsmen in the land.

⊙ He covered the interior of the temple with cedar and overlaid it with gold.

⊙ He commissioned intricate carvings to decorate the temple inside and out.

Are you starting to get the picture? He was dedicated to making this temple the be-all/end-all of houses for God (1 Kings 5:1–6:38).

Oh, by the way, he spent seven years on it.

Seven *years*.

And in that entire time, Solomon never wavered (that we know of) from the goal of building the temple. He was focused, and nothing was going to stand in his way. He and his people just went about doing the task, and when things got rough (and you know they did), they just kept on doing their task.

Dedication.

Napoleon has it. Do you?

What do you do when you're, say, painting a room? Do you tape everything off to make sure the paint doesn't get everywhere? Do you properly prepare the surface? Do you apply the paint with nice, even strokes to make sure you get even coverage? Do you allow the paint time to (

What about when you talk to a person about something important? Do you really make a point to listen to what they're saying? Do you think about the problems they're telling you? Do you put your own life on hold so you can offer some assistance to this person in need?

Would you spend three hours on something as inconsequential as the shading of an upper lip?

Maybe God hasn't called you to be a great artistic talent. But he does want you to give life your best, and if that means taking the time that something — or someone — needs, then take it.

Then your life will probably be the best drawing you've ever done.

Work from the heart for your real Master, for God.
Colossians 3:23

you have a sweet bike, and you're really good at hooking up with chicks.

So starts Napoleon's list of Pedro's qualifications to be class president. The next line is priceless: "Plus, you're like the only guy in school with a mustache."

All very presidential attributes, right?

To recap: Vote for Pedro because he rides a Sledgehammer, he builds a mean cake, and he hit puberty before everyone else. Oh, and thank you for your vote.

Okay, just for fun, let's examine Napoleon's very trivial list and see what positive conclusions we can draw. First, Pedro has a sweet bike, probably a bike most students don't have. That makes him an independent thinker. Fair enough?

Second, he's pretty good at hooking up with chicks, which, as we can see through his behavior toward Summer and Deb, makes him thoughtful. Third, he's the only guy in school with a mustache. Well, that's just code for "mature." So, for those of you keeping score at home, Pedro is:

⊙ Independent

⊙ Thoughtful

⊙ Mature

We already know Pedro's high points; let's try to think of some low ones. For starters, he isn't exactly the quickest-witted student in school. With his strange, cowboy-boot-influenced running style, he isn't going to win any track meets any time soon. And he isn't very good at finding his locker on the first day of school.

Now let's apply the same thinking as above and draw some conclusions from my list of drawbacks. Examining the list, we can determine that Pedro is not:

⊙ Verbose

⊙ Athletic

⊙ A navigator

Of the two sets of skills listed above, which is the better set for a class president to possess? I (Adam) know it's a stretch, but stick with me for a bit; I'm trying to make a point. When Pedro was still considering a run for president, Napoleon helped him identify his strengths so he could, in a sense, focus on those strengths.

Just take a look at his speech. He did his own thing, setting himself apart from Summer. He showcased some great ideas for helping the school out (instead of Summer's plans for pop machines and new cheerleading uniforms and her "chimini-changas" crack, which was a completely unnecessary jibe at Pedro's heritage), and he showed some maturity in his willingness to make a speech after Summer's enthusiastic reception. A less mature person would've cowered in fear at the thought of saying something unprepared and then not having a killer skit.

The point here is this: God has given us all certain gifts and talents; it's up to us to identify those and use them.

A friend and I were recently talking about his nine-year-old and seven-year-old sons and the current quandary he had with them. The older is more into books and reading and studying, while the younger is a more natural athlete, complete with the take-the-other-guy-down m necessary to compete at high levels.

My friend is finding it difficult for his older son to play sports, because the boy never does well in them. He just isn't gifted in that area. Dad is starting to realize this, so he's discovering other areas of competition where his son can excel. Dad is teaching his older son to play to his strengths.

There's a passage in the Bible that touches on this, too. In the apostle Paul's letter to the Ephesians, he talks about God's diversity in gift-giving, saying that some people are meant to be sent out as messengers, some people are meant to spread the good news abroad, and some are meant to stay back to shepherd and teach others (see Ephesians 4:11-13). Why? So that everyone will find their right place and we can all grow and mature together to become everything God wants us to be.

God is a diverse God, and he knew what he was doing when he gave out gifts and talents. What if everyone in the world of *Napoleon Dynamite* was just like Pedro? Or just like Napoleon? Or just like Deb? We all have different strengths and weaknesses, and we must learn to accept them, focusing on the strengths while minimizing the weaknesses.

Sometimes it's hard because we really want to be strong in a certain area that maybe is more of a weakness for us. There's nothing wrong with working hard to get there; but don't do it to the detriment of your actual strengths. God gave you that talent for a reason. Use it for him.

God's various gifts are handed out everywhere; but they all originate in God's Spirit.

1 Corinthians 12:4

Sweet! Plus, I could be your
bodyguard, too. Or, like,
secret service captain or whatever.

Napoleon's offer of service to Pedro, should Pedro win the presidency, was met with a certain amount of indifference. (Of course with Pedro, how can one tell indifference from excitement?) Maybe it is because Pedro already had his cousins with their sweet car to serve as bodyguards. Or maybe Pedro was counting on "holy santos," especially El Santo Niño de Atocha, who his Aunt Concha had seen. In any case, it seems Pedro was already protected. (This is cool: El Santo Niño de Atocha is the patron saint of those unjustly accused or imprisoned.)

How about you? Do you have a bodyguard? Could you use a secret service captain in your life? Or do you feel like you are all alone, with no one to watch over you? If you are a follower of Jesus, you can turn down Napoleon's offer — you already have a bodyguard.

Right now, you're probably thinking: "Please. If I was the president of the U.S., or maybe a celebrity, I'd need a bodyguard *in addition* to Jesus." True. But hear me out. What I (Jeff) am saying is figurative.

Let's visit Jesus as he is talking to his followers shortly before he was crucified. He's addressing this group of men and women who have been with him now for nearly three years, but in a much different way than before. Jesus keeps talking about going away, about not being seen by them any longer. Then he says things are not going to be pretty for these followers. They are going to be thrown out of the synagogues, hauled into court, imprisoned. Think these guys were scared? Do you think they would have readily accepted an offer of protection right then?

In the middle of this gloomy speech, Jesus gives them some good news. "I will talk to the Father, and he'll provide you another Friend so that you will always have someone with you" (John 14:16). The word Jesus used for this Friend was *Paraclete*, which means "one called to be alongside to help." Kind of sounds like a bodyguard, doesn't it? Only in this case, the helper was not there to guard bodies, but spirits.

Jesus was preparing his followers for tough times ahead and offered no promise that they would not suffer physically for being identified with him. But he did say their spirits, the part of us that will live forever, would be safe.

> "The Friend, the Holy Spirit whom the Father will send at my request, will make everything plain to you. He will remind you of all the things I have told you. I'm leaving you well and whole. That's my parting gift to you. Peace. I don't leave you the way you're used to being left — feeling abandoned, bereft. So don't be upset. Don't be distraught." (John 14:26-27)

Imagine having perfect peace on the inside, even while a storm rages around you on the outside. Friends abandon you. Classmates make fun of you. Those who consider themselves intellectually superior to you tell you why your beliefs are wrong. Yet you have peace in your spirit and don't give up.

Or you may be in a situation much worse. You might be in a nation where being a follower of Jesus is more than inconvenient in certain social circles. You may be in a place — and they are growing throughout the world at an alarming rate — where being identified as a Christian can cost you your property, life savings, career — or maybe your life. The persecution of Christians is greater now than at any time in history. This was foretold by Jesus, so we should not be surprised when it happens. And we can also count on the Friend promised by Jesus, the Holy Spirit, being with us to give us peace through anything we face.

Many hundreds of years ago, three young men — probably about the same age as Napoleon and Pedro — needed a bodyguard. Ordered to bow down to a statue of the king, and thus renounce the one true God, they refused and were ordered to be executed. A fire pit was heated so hot that the guards who forced these three young men toward it were devoured by the flames. The three were thrown into the fire, and the king rushed to watch them burn alive.

That was when the king's eyes were opened to the fact that he was not God. Those three young men, bound hand and foot and thrown into a raging furnace, were walking around freely, with no signs of even being a tad warm. Then the king noticed that there were not three, but four people in the furnace. And the fourth, the king said, looked like the son of God. Their bodyguard was with them, and the three young men were pulled out of the furnace and given promotions within the kingdom, all because they knew who was God and that God had their backs.

The Holy Spirit is the very nature of God within you to help and comfort you if you are a follower of Jesus. Even Napoleon, your secret service captain, can't offer that kind of protection!

"I will talk to the Father, and he'll provide you another Friend so that you will always have someone with you."

John 14:16

17

*I am 100% positive
she's my soul mate.*

It isn't a stretch to say that just about everyone in the developed world has wrestled with idea of a soul mate. No one is born married, so we've all done the whole meeting, getting-to-know-you, dating thing.

For Kip, that thing just happened to take place via the Internet. Chatting online with babes all day paid off for him; it was there that he met LaFawnduh. And after she paid him a visit, he became certain that she was *the* best thing that's ever happened to him.

How likely is it that your search for a soul mate follows this same path? Not very. Kip is, after all, a character in a while real life is often stranger than a movie, ppens like one. You aren't necessarily going to follow Kip's path to marital success (and really, if you want to do anything just because Kip does it . . . well, we need to talk), so that brings us back to this troublesome question of the soul mate.

Is there a soul mate out there for you? Is the person you're currently dating your soul mate? Will you ever meet your soul mate? Are you already married to your soul mate or did you miss the boat?

While these questions might have some validity, they aren't really the sort of questions you need to be asking. Instead, ask about yourself.

Are you a good soul mate for someone?

Keep that in mind as we examine Kip. LaFawnduh must have seen something in him or she wouldn't have made the bus trip to Preston. He must have offered something she liked, and vice versa. Kip saw something in her — or at least in her writing and her head-only photograph — that attracted him to her. They're such an odd pair that we get the feeling there must be something genuine there.

And then LaFawnduh's bus pulls into the station, and

we begin to see Kip change. For starters, he smiles for the first time in the movie (letting us see what we suspected: that he has braces). He lets her set aside his glasses. He willingly accepts her gift of enormous bling. He finally kicks off one of those awful canvas shoes.

Later on, we see a transformed Kip, one released from his outer nerdy trappings. He even changed his language choices along the same lines ("Peace out"). So the question becomes: Did Kip change who he was or did LaFawnduh's arrival merely bring out his inner "G"?

My money is on the latter. Let me elaborate: In my estimation, Kip's character remains constant despite his outward changes. When LaFawnduh first arrived, she became a catalyst for Kip to change his outer appearance, for him to experiment with a different style of dress and speech. But even without his glasses and polo shirts, we can see from Kip's conversation with Napoleon that he's the same guy.

Fast forward to their wedding. The changes Kip underwent in the film have lost their newness. He's decided he didn't want to tilt his style so far in the other direction, so the glasses are back and the bling is gone (except for that microphone). But through the changes, Kip, as a person, remained the same man he was when he started his first chat with LaFawnduh. And through it all, he's stayed in love with her, and she with him.

Because they never changed.

They were good soul mates for each other because they started out as good soul mates themselves.

I seriously doubt Kip sat down at his computer day after day after day hoping that someday he would meet someone exactly like LaFawnduh, and I'm sure it was likewise for her. Instead, Kip met her in a chat room and was himself, showing her through his own cheesy poetry how much she meant to him. And his grand singing gesture at the end of the movie drives the point home even further. He even mentions his love for technology in a song for his new wife. That's being true to yourself. That's being a good soul mate.

The Bible says a lot of things, but it's pretty thin when it comes to talking about molding other people into what you'd like them to be. And it doesn't really touch on the subject of "finding the right guy/girl."

Instead, it talks about you. Who you are.

God is much more concerned with you taking care of

yourself and becoming the person he wants you to be than with you finding your soul mate. The Bible uses language like "clay" and "potter" to describe our relationship to God (Isaiah 64:8), an indication that maybe, just maybe, he's in charge of the whole thing and that we are just what he makes of us.

So allow God to make something of you. Instead of being on the lookout for your soul mate, be looking inward, toward yourself, to see how you can become a better soul mate for someone someday. The same holds true if you're already married: laundry lists of ways your spouse can improve aren't exactly the way to go; instead, find ways you can improve yourself and become the best soul mate for them.

In the end, you are only responsible for yourself, and your search for a soul mate ends right at your very own door.

Peace out.

Still, GOD, you are our Father.
We're the clay and you're our potter:
All of us are what you made us.

Isaiah 64:8

You've been ruining everyone's lives and eating all our steak!

Ah, Uncle Rico. Crazy, crazy Uncle Rico. He's one of the more interesting characters in the movie because of his unwillingness to part with the past. He's very melancholy, reliving the glory days as a footballer. But worse, his selfish business pursuits haunt Napoleon and make for a rough life at school.

Think about it. Other than Randy's bullying, every hardship Napoleon encounters during the movie is brought about by Uncle Rico's selfishness in getting the sale. What little reputation Napoleon has gets tarnished more and more as Uncle Rico insults Napoleon's bladder problems (does he really wet his bed?), monetary status (in front of

117

Summer), punctuality (when he leaves Napoleon stranded in the van before the dance), and family life (when he gives Trisha and Summer the, ahem, flier).

But the straw that broke the camel's back was the call from Deb. You remember the scene. She calls Napoleon from a pay phone and chews him out for being a "shallow friend." She mentions Uncle Rico's name and Napoleon figures out the whole thing. (Looks like "stealth detective work" is another one of Napoleon's skills.) After Deb hangs up, Napoleon marches to the porch to tell Uncle Rico to pack it up.

Uncle Rico is nothing but trouble to Napoleon.

Just like Jesus promised.

Yes, Jesus said something about the Uncle Ricos of this world. You've had at least one — maybe more — in your life. And I'm not just talking about people who bug you. Situations, problems, illnesses, setbacks, financial crunches, relationship difficulties, arguments, stress, deadlines, uptight teachers, overflowing diapers . . . they're all little (or big) Uncle Ricos in your life.

Jesus called them difficulties. Trouble.

He said this is a godless world, and because of that, you

will have difficulties (see John 16:33).

There is no getting around Uncle Rico. He is going to show up at your house, and he will bring his big, ugly, orange van with him, whether you like it or not.

He will make you watch his video.

He will give you a bad reputation among your friends and acquaintances.

He will eat all your steak.

In the Old Testament, Joseph knew a little something about Uncle Rico — he had several Rico-like encounters in his life. His brothers hated him, so they dumped him in a pit to die. Then they thought they could make some money off him, so they sold him into Egyptian slavery. Joseph worked hard for his new master, achieved some notoriety, then was lied about and thrown into prison. He was there long enough to start running the place when he helped out a couple of the Pharaoh's servants who were stuck in prison with him. One of those servants promised to tell Pharaoh about Joseph's wrong imprisonment as soon as he was reinstated.

He forgot.

For two years.

Finally, his memory was jogged, and Joseph was released

from prison and promoted to second in command of Egypt. It would be easy to lose count of all the Uncle Ricos Joseph encountered in that very brief paraphrase of his story (if you want to read the whole thing, you'll find it in Genesis, chapters 37, 39-47). But he never let all his troubles get to him, and he never stopped trusting God to provide a way through the difficulties.

Back to Jesus. True, he promised there would be difficulties in this godless world, but he also promised something else right after that.

He said he'd already overcome the world.

Uncle Rico, it's time to go home. Pack up the video camera, put away the footballs, climb in your van, and get off my property.

I have called the cops on you.

Life experience tells us that Uncle Ricos don't automatically leave the second they arrive. Sometimes they hang around for a few days or weeks or years, attempting to assimilate themselves into our lives. But rest assured, Jesus has overcome the world and sees the squatter on your life known as Uncle Rico. When the time is right, he will be dispatched back to the empty field.

We all know this life will never be trouble-free. But, when God is in your corner (excuse the cliché), you have a way to cope with troubles when they barge into your kitchen and tuck a paper towel under the front of their shirt to keep off steak juice. Somehow, God makes it tolerable, gently reminding you of Jesus' words. Reminding you that he has overcome the world. Reminding you of an eternity without difficulties or troubles, one that awaits you.

"In this godless world you will continue to experience difficulties. But take heart! I've conquered the world."

John 16:33

Just tell them all their wildest dreams will come true if they vote for you.

Seems like everyone these days is daring to dream. Gone are the days when men wore hats, when they worked for the same company for thirty or forty-plus years, while their wives stayed home to raise the children and keep the house spotless and wear pearls and dresses. Maybe those days never really existed except on TV.

But dreams are a big part of the overall human conversation now. "What do you want to be when you grow up?" is no longer a question just for elementary school kids, and answers like "doctor," "firefighter," "astronaut," or "ballet dancer" are no longer gender-specific. We live in an unprecedented time when you pretty much have the opportunity to do just about anything you want to do, as long as it's legal.

And dreams don't stop with occupations. Most of us work for a living, so most of us automatically assign dreams to the way we provide for ourselves. But dreams can apply to other realms: We can dream of a certain family life or of being able to pursue a certain hobby. We may dream of playing professional sports or of being a rock star, and not because of the money those dreams would bring, but because of the fame. Like dreams themselves, the word "dream" has broad applications.

So then, that begs the question: What are your wildest dreams? You live in a society where those dreams are most likely possible; are you living them out? What would you be doing with your life if you absolutely knew you could not fail at it? Would your life be any different?

Here we have this amazing capacity to flex our dream muscles and make our wildest dreams happen, and yet so many of us aren't doing it. That's why Pedro's promise of wildest dreams coming true could carry so much weight

among the student body. That, and Napoleon's da
a fulfillment of wildest dreams, in a way), were
propel Pedro past Summer and to the presidency. Sweet.

Perhaps many people aren't seeing fulfilled dreams in their lives because they're looking to the wrong thing to fulfill them. David wrote in one of his psalms that it is God who gives the desires of the heart (see Psalm 37:4). It isn't a boss or a parent; it isn't a sibling or a child; it isn't an occupation or a hobby; it isn't a car or a house or a 52-inch plasma flat-screen TV or sweet dance grooves or any one particular thing or talent.

God is the one who makes our wildest dreams come true.

But there's a catch. If we back up and check out more of David's psalm, we see that there's more to it. We see that before he talks about God giving the desires of the heart, there's something we have to do: delight ourselves in God. In a sense, we have to "vote for him," but instead of just checking a box and being done with our part, we get to be fully involved, on staff with the administration and participating in daily briefings.

Fortunately for us, these things are a delight. A relationship with God is meant to be delightful, a joy, a wonder. Remember as a little child how delightful a trip to the ice cream shop was? Eating that single scoop of vanilla or chocolate or strawberry atop that sugar cone funnel—it didn't get any better. That's a shadow of the delight God wants us to have in our relationships with him.

But we so often get that part of the equation wrong, looking instead to delight ourselves in our desires, instead of in the God *who gives us those desires*. We expect the time machine to work without putting in the crystals, and then we get frustrated when all we get is a shock (okay, the time machine would never have worked anyway—bad analogy). A lamp won't illuminate anything if it isn't plugged into a working outlet. God is the source from which our desires will shine; expecting it the other way around only leads to disappointment.

And then there's another way of looking at it. Maybe, just maybe, people aren't seeing their dreams fulfilled because they're dreaming the wrong dreams. When David said God would give us the desires of the heart, maybe he was talking about God literally placing the desire in our hearts in the first place. If so, then delighting in God brings fulfillment

in two ways: Not only do we get to live our d[
get to live the *right* desires, the God-given ones.

Look at Napoleon. He spends the entire movie drawing animals and warriors and stuff. He draws because he has a desire to express himself creatively. However, while this desire is in the same vein, it is at a right angle to his actual talent: dancing. Dancing is a creative expression, but through a different art form, and it is the one Napoleon is actually best at.

When we delight ourselves in God (not saying Napoleon found his killer dance skills because he delighted in God, but you get the point), he directs us toward the desire that best matches our gifts and talents, as well as giving us a stage where we can see those desires happen in our lives. So dare to dream; just make sure you're dreaming in the right direction. And then all your wildest dreams will come true.

Keep company with GOD, get in on the best.
Psalm 37:4

What?! A flippin skit?! Why didn't anyone tell us about this?!

The Boy Scouts have possibly one of the most famous mottos in the world. You're probably already thinking of it right now, just from the mere mention of "Boy Scouts" and "motto" in the same sentence. Attribute it to good marketing — and good advice. "Be prepared" are the words that have inspired many a boy to tote around a pocketknife and a buttload of knowledge about the wilderness, just in case he ever needed them.

But preparedness, as you've no doubt already learned, isn't something you only need as a boy (or girl). You have to be prepared at work, in case your boss wants to take a

129

look at those latest sales figures. You have to be prepared at home, in case your toddler decides to give herself an impromptu oatmeal shampoo. You have to be prepared on the road, in case that car in front of you doesn't check the mirrors before changing lanes.

Being prepared is a fact of life. Napoleon and Pedro weren't officially prepared with a skit (especially something that would match the brilliant coordination of Summer's sign-language dance routine), but, as the movie tells us in exquisite detail, Napoleon saw the need and realized he was indeed prepared, even though he hadn't seen the need for that preparation in advance.

God has a thing or two to say about preparation, too, though he calls it something else. The apostle Paul was giving instruction to his young prodigy Timothy. He'd already written one letter to Timothy and was now wrapping up a second when he tells Timothy to keep on his watch (see 2 Timothy 4:2). Essentially, he's advising Timothy to be ready to say or do the right thing, no matter what situation may arise.

Sound familiar? When Napoleon bought *D-Qwon's Dance Grooves* from the thrift store, he had no idea it would propel him to stardom in front of his entire school. He simply took an interest in something, studied it, and then found that the skill was there when he needed to use it.

Good advice for life, to be sure. Your education shouldn't end when you get your last diploma. Being a lifelong student will not only give you that extra level of preparedness when you need it, but it will also enrich your life in ways you never dreamed. Plus, since you're deciding your own life's "curriculum," you get to study whatever you want.

But while that's good, it isn't really the type of preparation Paul's asking Timothy to do. Paul wanted to make sure Timothy was always ready, both in his mind and in his heart, to offer encouragement, or correction, or open rebuke — whatever he was called upon to give. If someone's tent-making business wasn't doing so well, he needed to be able to offer a verbal pick-me-up. If someone had misunderstood one of his sermons, he needed to be able to put them on the right track. If someone was intentionally doing wrong, he needed to be able to smack them with a loving rebuke.

This is the type of preparedness God wants us to possess. How many times have you been in the midst of a conversation, maybe with a friend or coworker telling you about a problem at home, and found yourself wishing you knew the right thing to say? Not knowing the *right* thing to say can often lead to saying the exact *wrong* thing and making a bad situation worse.

So how can you be prepared for that sort of situation? Well, it helps to be well-read, but since you can't read everything, you should probably choose your reading well, starting with the Bible. You can usually offer an answer from there, and if you're really stumped but are called upon to provide an answer, say a quick prayer and ask God for a little help. It worked for Pedro, who looks heavenward (and says a prayer, we assume) when he realizes his speech must wow the audience, who is wildly applauding Summer's speech.

God can give you the answers you need, both by answering your prayer and by speaking to you through his Word. You only need to ask him. And who better to ask than the one being in the whole universe who knows everything? Then you'll be ready for flippin' anything.

So proclaim the Message with intensity; keep on your watch. Challenge, warn, and urge your people. Don't ever quit. Just keep it simple.

2 Timothy 4:2

Listen to your heart.

That's what I do.

As Pedro is about to walk across a lonely stage to give his speech ("I'll just tell them I don't have anything to say"), Napoleon offers this great piece of advice. It is his last bit of dialogue for the rest of that entire scene. What we see is Napoleon — and the other characters — listening to their hearts.

⊙ Pedro goes on to give a speech after all, saying it would be a good idea to invite some "holy santos" (saints) to walk the school's hallways for protection and good luck.

⊙ Deb sees, from her heart, the true Napoleon, one who sticks up for his friends — even if it means public ridicule. She leads the applause and starts a standing ovation for Napoleon and Pedro.

⊙ Kip and LaFawnduh, true soul mates, listen to their hearts and board a bus for Detroit, where perhaps Kip asks her father's permission to marry LaFawnduh.

⊙ Grandma is back home, taking care of her boys and, of course, Tina.

⊙ Uncle Rico has followed his heart back to the wheat fields where he can endlessly relive 1982. And—surprise!—Tammy follows her heart back to him.

Most of all, we see Napoleon following his heart. With only minutes to prepare a skit, Napoleon takes a leap of faith and lands in the spotlight in front of the entire school. The skit/dance that ensues could only have come from his heart. If he had thought about all of his moves, about the rhythm of the music, about the what and why and how of his actions, he most likely would have been frozen in place, unable to move. Yet his heart took over, and the result was Napoleon free to be Napoleon.

God has much to say about your heart. "Heart" is

synonymous with "soul" — your nature, your i
with that in mind, heeding Napoleon's advice to
heart" could possibly lead to great results or a ro.... .....u wiin
ruin. It all depends on the condition of your heart. And the
condition most of us are in, we must admit, is not that great.

This is nothing new. Somewhere around 600 BC, a
young man named Jeremiah spoke a prophecy, words from
God meant for the people of Jeremiah's time. And they still
ring true today. Here is what God, through Jeremiah, had
to say about the human heart.

> The heart is hopelessly dark and deceitful,
> a puzzle that no one can figure out. But
> I, GOD, search the heart and examine the
> mind. I get to the heart of the human. I
> get to the root of things. I treat them as
> they really are, not as they pretend to be.
> (Jeremiah 17:9-10)

If that is the case, if it is true that our hearts are
hopelessly dark and deceitful, how can we follow our
hearts? That would be an invitation to disaster. Have you

ever done something you know you shouldn't do, but you couldn't stop yourself? Maybe you gossiped, or lied, or stole from your boss. Perhaps you would have joined Don and Summer and laughed at a nerd like Napoleon. These are all the actions of a dark and deceitful heart. It is the best we can do with the hearts we have. But there is hope.

David followed his heart. And once, that path led to adultery, murder, and the death of his infant son. It subsequently caused him to lose control of his kingdom and started events that led to hundreds of years of civil war in Israel. David saw that this was all his fault — he had run after what he thought was his own pleasure. When he honestly looked at his actions, and his motives for those actions, he pleaded with God for forgiveness. And, to be sure he did not follow the same path again, David asked God to create a new, clean heart in him, and to fill him with a "right" spirit (see Psalm 51:10, NRSV). We know that God answered David's prayer, for later in the Bible David is referred to as a man after God's own heart (as recorded in Acts 13).

So, yes, heed Napoleon's advice and follow your heart. But do that after you have asked God to create a new, clean heart in you. It is only with a God-made heart that you can freely dance across the stage.

> *The heart is hopelessly dark and deceitful, a puzzle that no one can figure out. But I, GOD, search the heart and examine the mind. I get to the heart of the human. I get to the root of things. I treat them as they really are, not as they pretend to be.*
>
> Jeremiah 17:9-10

Wanna play me?

Let's recap the parts of the movie that brought us to this phrase:

⊙ In his selfish pursuit for a sale, Uncle Rico lied to Deb and put words in Napoleon's mouth that were never said.

⊙ Deb then called Napoleon and told him he was "a shallow friend."

⊙ Napoleon got his groove on for Pedro's skit.

⊙ Deb saw the actual depths of Napoleon's friendship skills.

⊙ Deb met Napoleon on the tetherball court for a spirited round of everyone's favorite playground game, set to some pretty sweet eighties music.

Something to notice here: When Deb called Napoleon and broke off their friendship, Napoleon could've done what most of us would have done. He could've frantically put the blame back on Uncle Rico, demanding that he'd been falsely accused. But instead, he just kept quiet.

What brought Deb to the tetherball pole that day wasn't anything Napoleon said — it was what he did. She recognized his selfless act for his friend, his willingness to make a fool of himself in front of the whole school. When Napoleon worked it out on the dance floor, Deb cheered and saw him for who he truly was — a kind, if slightly bizarre guy who cares for his friends.

And looking at it from Napoleon's angle, I doubt he thought as he stepped hurriedly on stage, *This is going to get me back in with Deb*. He was just doing what needed to be done for the moment; Deb's turnaround was a by-product of that. So, in doing a favor for Pedro, Napoleon actually solidified *two* friendships.

We can all learn a thing or two from the book of Proverbs, and the book has some interesting things to say about friendships. Most of it was written by King Solomon, who is widely known as the wisest man who ever lived, a man who ruled his subjects with God-given wisdom. This guy was really, really smart and had a lock on practical advice for people.

One of the proverbs Solomon wrote touches on this exact moment in Napoleon's life. In Proverbs 18:19, we see this admonition: "Do a favor and win a friend forever; nothing can untie that bond."

You might even say that bond is tightly tethered. It isn't going anywhere, no matter how many times it gets hit around that pole.

But back to Deb's phone call. When she chewed Napoleon out (in her own reserved way), he didn't sputter in protest and he didn't get angry. He simply followed his heart (his words, not mine) and did a favor for his friend Pedro. Deb saw that favor and realized that her "shallow friend" comment was way off—Napoleon's friendship might, in fact, be as deep as they come.

Actions speak louder than words, as the saying goes.

No need for Napoleon to *say* something when *doing* something will in turn say more than anything that would come out of his mouth.

Either say or do.

See, unnecessary talking gets you nowhere. James (Jesus' brother) knew this and wrote about it in a letter targeted toward Jews scattered throughout the known world. Here's what he had to say about talking:

> This is scary: You can tame a tiger, but you can't tame the tongue — it's never been done. The tongue runs wild, a wanton killer. With our tongues we bless God our Father; with the same tongues we curse the very men and women he made in his image. (James 3:7-11)

You get the point — talk is cheap and easy and dangerous. It's just too convenient to let our tongues waggle and say whatever. Action — that's what James recommends:

> Lead with your ears, follow up with your tongue, and let anger straggle along in the rear. . . . Don't fool yourself into thinking that you are a listener when you are anything but, letting the Word go in one ear and out the other. Act on what you hear! (James 1:19,22)

There are times when a defense of your actions — or lack of them — might be necessary to clear up a misunderstanding or miscommunication. But here's something to try the next time you find yourself on the business end of a damaged relationship:

Be quiet.

Astonishing, I know. Care to take it a step further?

Listen.

Being quiet and listening, the real-world equivalents of Napoleon's dance. By closing your mouth and opening your ears in the midst of an argument, you show the other person that you care enough to control your knee-jerk self-defense. You show that you're actually attempting to see things from their point of view, to hear what they have to say.

You're taming the liger. I mean tiger.

And then comes the hard part. Acknowledge that, yes, they do have a point. Most of the time, arguing happens because one party assumes the other's opinion is invalid — but seldom is this ever true. If you can take an unblinking look at the situation, you'll generally see that both of you have valid points, just not ones that agree with each other. By simply acknowledging the other person's viewpoint, you've already begun to mend the break between you.

You don't have to go to extravagant lengths and perform in front of the whole school; just by "leading with your ears," you're taming the liger of your tongue and forming the initial knots of a friendship tether that can only wrap tighter and tighter.

> *This is scary: You can tame a tiger, but you can't tame the tongue — it's never been done. The tongue runs wild, a wanton killer. With our tongues we bless God our Father; with the same tongues we curse the very men and women he made in his image.*
>
> James 3:7-11

I just got done taming a wild honeymoon stallion for you guys.

Okay, I (Jeff) seriously doubt a stallion was on Kip and LaFawnduh's wedding registry. And why didn't Napoleon list "taming wild horses" among his skills? That one would go right up there with bow-hunting, numchuks, and computer-hacking.

Kip and LaFawnduh mounted the stallion and rode off to begin their life together as husband and wife. Yet no matter how great Napoleon's horse-training skills were, that stallion would no doubt still exhibit signs of wildness along the trail. There would be times when, no matter how

145

hard they pulled on the reins, the horse would go where he wanted to go, not where Kip and LaFawnduh had planned to go.

Life, it seems, is not a tamed stallion. Oftentimes, life is wild and out of our control. And no amount of yanking on the reins will get us back in control. We often feel like we are simply hanging on, hoping to survive life. Some scenarios:

⊙ You love your job, especially after your promotion. You actually enjoy going to work every day, those who work for you are your friends, and that raise allowed you to finally buy a house and that sports car you always wanted. Then there is a merger, a reconfiguration, and the layoffs begin.

⊙ This is the one — THE one. You have been dating each other for months now, have worked through the bumps in the road, and have been talking about the best time of year for a wedding. Then there is a strained phone call — "We need to talk."

⊙ A beautiful day for a drive, nary a cloud in the sky. A truck comes out of nowhere. You survive the collision, but a wheelchair is all you will be driving from now on.

These are, admittedly, extreme examples of losing control of life. But think of the everyday situations where you feel helpless. A quiz in class you weren't expecting. A question asked by a customer that you should be able to answer, but can't. An argument with your spouse, parents, or best friend. Throwing your best stuff, only to have the batters hit the ball like it is on a tee.

The stallion is riding wild, and you have no way to bring it under control.

Fortunately, there is one who can tame the wildest, most out-of-control situation you can imagine. There is no horse he cannot break, and nothing you will face in your life that he cannot work out for your good.

Jesus had spent the day teaching the crowds that came to him. Then he gathered up his close followers, his special students, and they got into a boat to cross the sea. Jesus, being totally in control, settled back for a nap. He had barely fallen asleep when the winds picked up. The waves rocked the boat mercilessly. They stood straight up on one wave, then rushed back down another. Water filled the boat faster than they could bail it out with buckets. Rowing was useless — it was all they could do to hang on, to not fall overboard.

Through all of this, Jesus slept.

Those in the boat with him shook him awake. "Jesus, we're sinking! We are going to drown! Do something!" He did.

"Awake now, he told the wind to pipe down and said to the sea, 'Quiet! Settle down!' The wind ran out of breath; the sea became smooth as glass" (Mark 4:39). Jesus took control of an out-of-control situation, a storm, and all were safe.

Some time later, Jesus told these same followers to get in a boat and cross the sea, this time without him there. Once again, in the middle of the water, a storm took control of their lives. Wind, waves, water — none of which they could tame. Just when it seemed all was lost, they saw a ghost walking on the water. No, not a ghost. It was Jesus. And as he walked toward them, the storm calmed. He got in their boat and saw them safely to shore.

Jesus, the master of storms, the ultimate wild-stallion tamer. He wants to calm your storms, bring your life under his control. He will set you on a tamed honeymoon stallion and put you on a course in life with adventures over every hill. And even when it seems he is late to arrive — just like Napoleon at the Wedding of the Century — know that he will always come at just the right time.

"Quiet! Settle down!" The wind ran out of breath; the sea became smooth as glass.

Mark 4:39

I hope you guys' experiences are unforgettable.

Who ever thought of taming a wild stallion for a honeymoon present? For that matter, who ever thought of writing a devotional based on a quirky comedy? *Napoleon Dynamite* did not win any Oscars. It will never be considered one of the great movies like *Casablanca*, *It's a Wonderful Life*, or *Gone with the Wind*. *Napoleon Dynamite* is more than that. It is a celebration of the ordinary. It is a statement that average, everyday life can be an adventure you will never forget.

We have looked at life through the eyes of Napoleon, Pedro, Kip, Deb, and Uncle Rico. They all have their weaknesses and strengths, just like we all do. They wish

151

for a better past; they long for a better future; they struggle with the present. *Napoleon Dynamite* caught us all by surprise by reminding us of ourselves. This is not a movie with actors playing someone we could never be, nor would we even meet in real life. This is a clip from our everyday, very real-life experiences. And some of those experiences are ones we want to forget, like getting body-slammed into a locker or laughed at as we give our current-events speech in front of the whole class.

What we want to leave you with, however, is a blessing to live a life full of unforgettable experiences. Jesus calls it "abundant life," and he says it is the kind of life he came to offer to us all. "A thief is only there to steal and kill and destroy. I came so they can have real and eternal life, more and better life than they ever dreamed of" (John 10:10).

The thief Jesus is referring to in this passage is, of all things, religion. It is the endless laws and traditions that were heaped on the people by religious leaders during the time of Jesus. We have the same struggles facing us today. We want to codify what needs to be lived out from our hearts. Jesus knows that rules and regulations steal life like a thief. The life he offers is free and abundant, better than we could ever dream of. And this life is never-ending. We can have this throughout eternity!

If Napoleon had only lived according to expectations, he never would have taken the stage to dance Pedro into the presidency of their school. The "rules" of Preston High School required nerds like Napoleon to not ask "cool" girls out on dates. That was okay — Napoleon gained a true friend in Deb. So when it came time for a wedding gift for Kip and LaFawnduh, Napoleon did not check their registry and run out to the mall to buy them a Crock Pot or electric skillet. He listened to his heart — and gave a wild stallion that he tamed. Along with the horse he gave an even greater gift — his blessing for the newlyweds to live an unforgettable life together.

And that is where we want to leave you. We hope you have had as much fun reading these devotions as we have had writing them. We have not tried to overspiritualize what is meant to be only a fun movie. But we have taken hold of the fun and tried to apply it in a way that will enrich your life. God has a great, abundant life in store for you. Live it to its fullest. We hope you guys' experiences are unforgettable!

"I came so they can have real and eternal life, more and better life than they ever dreamed of."

John 10:10

GLOSSARY

NAPOLEON DEFINED: A GLOSSARY

Air. A measure of distance, usually used to determine height achieved from sweet jumps. Maximum amount of air allowed is, like, three feet.

Bad Boys. Flowing, colorful cotton pants worn by those with a disciplined image. No one wants a roundhouse kick to the face from the party wearing them. Also good for stowing borrowed tots to eat later in class.

Bass. A delicious fish, sometimes used as a peace offering between friends.

Big J's. A great place to eat. Makes stirrable milkshakes and greasy onion rings. Served in Styrofoam; not environmentally conscious.

Bodaggit. Derisive name directed at an especially despised person. Often accompanied by large citrus fruit hurled at same.

Boondoggle. Home-woven handicraft, usually presented in keychain form. A must-have for this season's fashion, though any person or persons who have attended Scout Camp may already possess a infinity of them. Also an excellent way to spread political messages.

Buddy System. Method of self defense wherein you stop flyin' solo and have somebody watching your back at all times.

ChapStick. Petroleum-based lip balm, usually applied when one's lips hurt real bad. To determine the location of ChapStick, consult the school nurse, who has, like, five sticks in her drawer.

Chat Room. Important meeting place with rigid usage times that absolutely cannot be missed. Can last up to three, four hours maybe. Also, a place for dating couples (see **Pretty Serious**).

College. Where your mom goes.

Crystals. Necessary for all attempts at time travel.

Dance, The. After-hours, high school social function wherein male students ask female students to attend with them via a creative method (i.e. cake-building, upper-lip-shading, etc.). Also a place where participants have a killer time.

Decoded. Especially undesirable condition of human waste.

Dreams, Wildest. What will come true if you vote for Pedro.

Dunes, The. Naturally occurring waves of sand, often ridden upon by grandmothers on all-terrain vehicles. Capable of breaking said grandmother's coccyx.

Egg. Versatile lunch food. Can be eaten hard-boiled by itself or in salad form on sandwiches. Can also be added raw to orange juice. Best eaten outside in the presence of flies.

Five Seconds. Approximate amount of time needed to make 120 bucks.

Gangs. Ragtag bands of students that populate certain schools by the buttload. Most gangs eagerly desire members who are pretty good with a bowstaff.

"Gosh!" Exclamation of choice. Used specifically to add emphasis to the end of a frustrated statement.

Gum. Shredded confection consumed in public school bathrooms during formal occasions. Grape flavor recommended.

Ham. Llama food.

Happy Hands Club. School-based group with heavy emphasis on dramatic song interpretation. Utilizes the latest in boombox technology to enhance their sign language skills. Tacitly say that love is a flower.

Holy Santos. Saints brought to the school to guard the hallway and bring the school good luck. El Santo Niño de Atocha is a good one, as can be testified by the eyewitness sighting of said saint by Aunt Concha.

"Idiot!" Expression of disapproval with the person to whom it is directed.

Liger. A lion and a tiger mixed, bred for its skills in magic. Pretty much a favorite animal.

Lip, Upper. When drawing, a difficult portion of the face to shade. Can take, like, three hours. When done properly, it results in the best drawing the artist has ever done.

Locker. Metallic closet often found lining school hallways. Difficult for new students to locate. The locker has many uses, primarily as a container of equipment and/or numchuks, though there is usually not enough room to fit both. Exterior can be used as a display of political-themed fliers or as an impromptu weapon for over-large school bullies.

Milk. Popular dairy-based drink, obtained from cows. Can be defiled with bleach and/or a cow that got into an onion patch, among other things (See **Whole**).

Mustache. Presidential qualification and sign of maturity. Gifted mustache-havers can grow one in a couple of days, and there is generally only one mustachioed student per school.

Nachos. Snack food made from freakin' chips and a large amount of grated cheese. Often the cause of extreme busyness in the person making them.

Name Tags. Small identification badges that indicate the wearer has all the answers. Especially effective if they have the wearer's picture on them, all laminated and whatnot, thereby making them look legit.

Nessie. Informal name for the legendary Loch Ness Monster. Nessie's ability to thwart destruction at the hands of Japanese scientists makes her our underwater ally.

NuPont. Brand of nearly indestructible fiber-woven bowls. Available in 24- and 32-piece sets, often with free mini-sailboats. Strong young bucks cannot break them, but big orange vans can.

Pegasus. Winged, mythical horse known to cross the road in front of bedroom doors.

Pigskin. Oblate spheroid that can be thrown up to a quarter of a mile in distance, but only during the year 1982. Perfect for throwing at video cameras and over mountains.

Piñata. Party favor that sometimes bears a resemblance to a political opponent. Frowned upon in Idaho; done in Mexico all the time.

Pretty Serious. Dating condition of couples who chat online for, like, two hours a day (see **T.O.ed**).

Protection. What Pedro offers, usually in the form of severe glances from his cousins with all the sweet hookups.

Quesa-dilluh. Less-than-desirable food item, usually eaten after someone else has consumed all the freakin' chips. Quesa-dilluhs must be prepared by the eventual eater and are especially undesirable when they've been danged.

Reflexes. Skill required of any persons training to be a cage fighter, many of whom aspire to attain the reflexes of a puma.

Ride, My. What's in your driveway.

Season. Important factor for determining proper wig usage. Also tied directly to whether said wig looks like a medieval warrior.

School Nurse. Medically trained person on staff at school. Doesn't know anything.

Sensei. Licensed instructor of Rex Kwon Do. Must be bowed to upon approach.

Skills. Qualities in males desired by females as a condition of the female bestowing them with boyfriendhood. Notable skills include numchuk skills, bow-hunting skills, or computer-hacking skills.

Skit. A surprise solo or group performance after a speech that often results in several moves being busted and/or grooves being gotten on.

Sledgehammer. Desirable transportation to/from school. Often found with shocks, pegs, and a seldom-mentioned tattered Mexican flag. Any owner of a Sledgehammer is considered lucky.

Sleeves. Part of a formal gown, usually homemade. Often classified as real big and liked by members of the opposing gender for that very reason.

Soft Around The Edges. Photographical condition easily obtained by hanging a nice, soft, pink sheet, then wrapping the subject to be photographed in some foam or something billowy. It particularly occurs with the fan going and some tinsel hung from above.

Soul Mate. 100 percent positively *the* best thing that ever happened to you.

Sports Drink. Red-dyed hydration beverage that restores necessary minerals to the body and T-shirt after much practicing of some dance moves.

State. Championship that could've been taken in 1982, had coach put the correct player in the game during the fourth quarter.

Steak. Meat product consumed in large quantities by selfish, melancholy uncles.

Stings. The condition of a neck after it has been wrung by the school bully. Condition heightened if a mole on the neck has been ripped off.

Suit. Apparel item found in thrift stores. Noteworthy suits are generally from a bygone era and look pretty sweet and/ or awesome and/or incredible.

"Sweet!" Exclamation of extreme approval of recently delivered news and/or developments. Intended to represent the lack of sourness and/or bitterness of said news/developments. Similar in usage to, but completely different from, **"Yes!"**

Talons, Large. As-yet-undetermined part of a chicken.

Tetherball. Pretty much the best playground game ever. Excellent play requires skills like side-kicking and exclaiming "Yesssssss" multiple times in a row.

T.O.ed. Condition similar to frustration when an online babe you're getting pretty serious with has not sent a full body shot (see **Pretty Serious**).

Tots. Potato-based, cylindrical side item served at lunchtime. Can also be eaten cold as a mid-class snack. Great for sharing; extremely portable (see **Bad Boys**). Delicate in texture, tots can be rendered inedible with a simple kick.

Trapper Keeper. Multipurpose, notebook-style container. Usually decorated with retro-futuristic space motif. Excellent carrier of death-defying action figures.

Trisha. My woman I'm taking to the dance.

Unicorn. Mythical, one-horned creature, sometimes seen with wings, always seen in one-dimensional form. Known for its ability to create visible flatulence.

Video, Home. Boring home movie, the plot of which consists of determining which football thrown at the camera will strike it. Considered by some to be the worst video ever made, though no one can even know that.

Video, Purchased. Exciting instructional video for those who desire to get their groove on. Hosted by D-Qwon.

Whole. What you could be drinking, if you wanted to (see **Milk**).

Wolverine. Vicious beast known to attack relatives in packs of, like, fifty. Wily and elusive, wolverines are best eliminated using a freakin' 12-gauge.

"Yes!" Expression of extreme pleasure in one's performance.

RECIPES

RECIPES FROM THE KITCHEN OF

Napoleon Dynamite

Appetizers

Kip's Nachos

Every day I come home from school to find Kip has eaten all the freakin' chips. He does like flippin' nothing all day. He says he needs the chips for energy as he trains to be a cage fighter, but he's got like the worst reflexes of all time.

Kip makes nachos this way. Dump a bunch of chips on a plate, then grate cheese on top of them. Use real cheese, not that fake processed cheese stuff. That's gross.

Put the plate into the microwave and warm it up until the cheese is melted. Eat with a glass of whole milk.

Dang Quesa-dilluh

Sometimes when Grandma goes away, or we're out of steaks, I make a quesa-dilluh. I have pretty good quesa-dilluh skills, pretty much the best that I know of. Here is how you do it.

Get a frying pan and put some cooking oil in it, then heat it over medium heat. Take a tortilla and spread sour cream on one side. Then get a can of chicken and put all the chicken on top of the sour cream. You can also put tomatoes, or peppers, on the tortilla. Then put on a bunch of grated cheese, and put another tortilla on top of all of this. Put the whole thing into the frying pan. Cook it for a little while on one side, then turn it over for a little more time. Cut it into pieces with a pizza cutter.

Meat and Poultry

Steak

Steak comes from cows. I learned this when I was real young by watching Lyle shoot a cow and the next day come to our house with a bunch of steaks. He still does that, I guess. Steaks are like my favorite food, except when Uncle Rico throws them like a football at me. He ruins my life! Gosh!

Grandma makes steaks this way. She heats a frying pan on the stove and puts some butter in it. When the butter starts to hiss, she puts the steak in the pan. After about three or ten minutes or something, she flips it over. Then she takes it out and puts it on a plate. I like to put ketchup on my steak.

Of course, it is sometimes hard to eat a steak sitting on the front porch. The cows in the field across the street come up to the fence and look at me like I'm eating one of their friends or something. So I just get up and go eat on the couch where they can't see me.

Delicious Bass

The first step in cooking a delicious bass is catching a delicious bass. What the heck is the difference between a delicious bass and a crappy bass? You catch a delicious bass using artificial bait. Would you want to eat something that has been eating worms? That's gross!

So go catch a delicious bass using plastic worms. Wrap it up and bring it home. Stop and play me in tetherball if you want.

You can clean the fish yourself, or pay someone to do it for you. I'm not going to describe how to clean a fish, because that's sicker than using ChapStick from the school nurse.

Next, build a fire. You can build the fire in a fireplace, or in a fire pit in the backyard. Or in a grill. Let the fire die down to the hot coal stage. While you are waiting for the flames to go down, tear a large sheet of aluminum foil. Place the bass in the middle of the foil, and pull all of the sides up around the bass. The bass will look like it is at the bottom of a boat of tinfoil. Melt about a tablespoon of butter in the microwave. Pour it over the bass. Take a pinch of dill spice and sprinkle it over the fish. Then fold the tinfoil over the top of the bass, sealing all the edges.

Drop the fish right into the fire. Listen to the butter and the fish hiss and pop. Flippin' sweet! Then, after five or eight minutes, turn the fishy tinfoil packet over, using barbecue tongs or something like that. Let it cook two or three more minutes, take it out of the fire, and let it cool for about three minutes. You can eat it right out of the foil if you want to. That way you don't have as many dishes to wash after dinner. Sweet.

Eggs

I don't eat eggs anymore, not since I helped move 8,000 chickens into a new coop. The farmer fed us hard-boiled eggs for lunch, and made us drink orange juice with raw eggs. Gross! I seriously almost threw up everywhere. And then he paid me in change, like, six dollars, which came to like a dollar an hour. I'll never eat eggs again.

Vegetables

Tots

Tots are vegetables, which you are supposed to eat a lot of. I like the tots they make at school pretty good I guess. If you can find someone who doesn't like tots, you can take his and save them until later when you're hungry again.

Grandma sometimes makes tots at home. Here is how you do it. You take the tots out of the bag in the freezer and dump them on a cookie sheet. Heat the oven to like 350 or 400 degrees and put the tots in the oven. You want them to cook until they are crispy, which takes flippin' forever. Like twenty minutes or something.

Tots are good to eat with steak. Tots and nachos are ok, but it's like all vegetables for dinner. So try to have some steak with your tots so you have a balanced meal.

Desserts

Building a Cake

If you want to impress a girl — ask her to a dance or something — do what my friend Pedro does. Build her a cake. It isn't as hard as you might think.

First, go to the store and buy a box of cake mix and a can of icing. You might think you can build a better cake than

Duncan Hines, but they've been doing it for, like, infinity years.

Follow the directions on the box. Mix all the stuff together, then pour most of it into a cake pan. You need to save some of it in the bowl to lick out with the spatula.

After you bake it in the oven, let it cool. If you try to put the icing on while the cake is still hot, all you will get is runny icing and a sick pile of crap. No girl is going to go to a dance with you if you give her a cake like that. Pedro would know. He's good at picking up chicks.

Pedro likes to leave the finished cake on the girl's front porch with a note, then ring the doorbell and run. That's okay, I guess. But I prefer the straight approach method. Just stand there with the cake and ask her if she wants to go to the dance with you. That way, if she says "no," you can keep the cake and eat it yourself.

Beverages

Whole vs. 1% Milk

A lot of people drink 1% milk because they think they won't get as fat. But think about it. If you are drinking 1% milk, then what is the other 99%? It might be something that would make you even fatter than drinking whole milk.

I prefer whole milk, unless of course the cow got into an onion patch. Then just give me some ice-cold sports drink straight from the bottle.

DISCUSSION

TAMING A LIGER
DISCUSSION GUIDE

Topic: Family Life

1. Napoleon and his brother are being raised by their grandmother. What do you suppose happened to their parents? Why?

2. Napoleon and Kip have an interesting relationship as brothers. Can you or your siblings relate to their relationship?

3. Napoleon and Kip's grandmother was not being honest with them about where she was and who she was with. How important is honesty among families? Have you ever held something back from a family member? Why?

4. Kip spends more time online than he does with his brother. Do you have anything that keeps you from spending time with your family? Do any of your family members have anything that keeps them from spending time with you? How do you feel about this?

5. Uncle Rico unknowingly ruins Napoleon's life by running his mouth and generally being intrusive. Which of these characters do you most relate to? Why?

Topic: School Life

1. Napoleon spends much of the movie being mocked or bullied. Can you relate?

2. Napoleon and Pedro become friends through a seeming coincidence. Do you have a close friend that you met in the same way? How did you become close? What keeps you close?

3. Summer and Don are the stereotypical "popular" kids at Napoleon's high school. How do you suppose they got that way? Who or what determines a student's popularity at your school?

4. Deb sits all alone in the lunchroom. Are there people in your school like that? Have you ever attempted to offer friendship to them? What happened?

5. Summer thinks she's a shoo-in for the presidency because of her popularity, since she certainly didn't have a well-thought-out plan for the school. Do you see

instances in your school or life where you make choices based on popularity instead of content? Why?

6. The Dance: Who do you relate to more? The people dancing or Napoleon, Pedro, and Deb standing on the outside?

Topic: Future Aspirations

1. Deb is selling home-woven handicrafts and glamour shots as a way to earn money for college. Can you relate to her work ethic? Why or why not?

2. In your opinion, what prompted Napoleon to purchase the dancing video? Why?

3. Uncle Rico's future aspirations involve changing the past. Do you have anything in your past you wished you could change? Name three ways you can move forward instead of looking backward.

4. Napoleon's skill set doesn't necessarily line up with the average person's. What sort of career do you think Napoleon could have using his given skills? What about you — what sort of skills do you have and what sort of career do they lend themselves to?

5. Kip and LaFawnduh end the movie riding off into their future together. What sort of future do you think their relationship holds? Why?

Topic: Dating

1. Pedro decided to ask Summer to the dance by building her a cake. Have you ever gone to such great lengths to show affection to someone? How was it received? How did you feel about that reception?

2. Kip meets his soul mate online. How do you feel about Internet dating? Why?

3. Napoleon passes off the girl in the glamour shots photo as his girlfriend. Napoleon and Kip's grandmother kept her boyfriend a secret. Have you ever lied about a relationship you did or did not have? Why?

4. Pedro's first question about Napoleon's supposed girlfriend was, "Is she hot?" Why is appearance such a common criterion for dating? Which is more important: looks or personality? Why?

5. Uncle Rico feels like his coach's error in 1982 has cost him a soul mate. Can you relate to this? Do you feel

like someone else has caused you to miss out on a potentially great relationship? Why or why not?

6. Napoleon and Deb are "just friends," but we can tell they have affection for one another. Is there anyone in your life you're "just friends" with? What has kept you that way? Some say being "just friends" is the best way to start a relationship. What do you think?

Topic: God

1. Which character in the movie comes the closest to reflecting the character of Christ? Why do you think so?

2. What do you suppose God makes of Napoleon's fantastical imagination?

3. Pedro prays before his speech. Name a recent incident where you prayed before a big event. What happened?

4. Pedro's house is covered with religious symbols, and he even sports a cross necklace. How bold are you about your relationship with God?

5. Kip talks about LaFawnduh being his soul mate. Do you believe God gives everyone a single soul mate? Why or why not?

ABOUT THE AUTHORS

Adam Palmer is the senior copywriter for a faith-based marketing/promotions company in Tulsa, Oklahoma. His work has appeared in *Relevant, 7Ball, Christian Retailing, Ministries Today,* and the *Refuel Biblezine.* Adam lives in Tulsa, Oklahoma, with his wife and children.

Jeff Dunn has been a contributing writer and developmental editor of a number of books including *Cracking da Vinci's Code* and the Christy Award-winning novel, *A Place Called Wiregrass.* Jeff and his wife, Kathy, live in Tulsa, Oklahoma, with their children.

Two pages later . . .

HABIT

Becoming Who We Are (Part 2)

Spent needles, cigarette butts, spitting bits of fingernail, toilet seats in the upright position . . . For some reason, when I hear the word *habit* my head naturally inserts *bad* in front of it. Don't think ill of me, please. In my defense, I just took a quick survey of those sitting within the proximity of my voice in Barnes & Noble and four out of five said "bad" when I asked what they thought of when they heard the word *habit*. I feel better. So . . . I hear *habit* and I think of things we human beings do that I perceive are not particularly positive. According to my thoroughly unscientific bookstore survey, odds are you do, too. Habits like drinking milk from the carton, cussing, buying Top 40 music, killing things,

191

grinding teeth, clicking a pen over and over and over, cleaning ears with sharp instruments like, say, keys or a light saber, burning things that look flammable, sleeping while driving. It's incredible the things that become habitual.

I sucked my thumb as a kid, long after I became aware that it was embarrassing to do so. I had been told and told to refrain, and I did not. I had been told it would give me buckteeth, but I sucked on. One morning a trip to the pharmacy commenced for the purchase of a horribly bitter liquid that had the appearance of clear fingernail polish but whose sadistic hidden intent was to break strong-willed kids of their thumb-sucking habits. My mom gave me money and waited in the car as I completed the transaction with our family pharmacist friend. The objective here was trauma. You don't give a kindergartener cash money and send them wandering into a pharmacy unless you are hoping to make a durable impression. I couldn't see over the counter. I just said my name and handed the guy in white the pretty green paper with the strange smell. He handed me a bag full of fright. That night my parents and I ceremoniously applied the liquid to both thumbnails. In a matter of days I had developed a small amount of love for this liquid. Sure it was acidly pungent and I'm certain it would overpower weaker children and bring them to submission but I . . . I would not bend. I would suck my thumb and grow buckteeth.